COW WOMAN
of Akutan

An EXTRAORDINARY, COMPELLING
Story of a UNIQUE ALASKA ADVENTURE

BY JOAN BROWN DODD

PO Box 221974 Anchorage, Alaska 99522-1974
books@publicationconsultants.com—www.publicationconsultants.com

ISBN 978-1-59433-479-5
eBook ISBN 978-1-59433-480-1
Library of Congress Catalog Card Number: 2014940558

Manufactured in the United States of America.

Dedication

Dedicated to the memories of Charlie Brown (1930-1999) and Hans Radtke (1935-1996) without whom my adventure would not be possible.

Acknowledgements

I am indebted to the excellent editorial assistance of James Engelhardt, Dawn Marano, and Rebecca Davis for their invaluable professional critiques. Independent of each other they saw the potential human interest of my story and offered me great encouragement. I also thank some of my Akutan friends for jogging my memory regarding incidents and dates that go back almost 50 years. Specifically helpful were Tina Kudrin Gauen, Alice Tcheripanoff, Moses Tcheripanoff, and Zenia Borenin. I know there were others and I hope this story will be a way of thanking the people of Akutan for being there when my family so desperately needed them.

Contents

Author's Note

In August of 2001 I received an improperly addressed letter of inquiry about some wild Hereford cows on Akutan Island in the Aleutians, off the coast of Alaska. The address did not include a post office box number. When that number was missing, often the post office returned the letter to the sender, even though Homer is a small town in Alaska. A real estate office where I'd once worked, Gold Rush Realty, was used as the address, but it had closed almost sixteen years before. Even with this improbable address, some thoughtful employee who may have recognized my name put the letter in the box I'd had since 1973.

This is the incorrect mailing address of the letter that I received thirty-one years after leaving the island.

Joan Brown
Gold Rush Realty
Homer, Alaska

This is the letter.

July 26, 2001

Dear Ms. Brown,

Your name was mentioned to me by several residents of Akutan as one of the persons who was involved in an attempt to introduce cattle to the island some years ago. Beyond that bare information, people's recollections differ and there is no consensus as to when or how this occurred. In my past six months on the scenic isle of Akutan, I have twice observed some of the cattle (or probably their descendants) that you and your husband brought here: they seem relatively healthy though through inbreeding they appear to come from the shallow end of the gene pool. As a transplanted Montana rancher I am very interested in any details, pictures, recollections, memories or tales you may have concerning these critters.

> Sincerely,
> Doug Dodd
> Box 9
> Akutan, AK 99553

I was surprised to learn that so many years later there was evidence that enough of the original cows had survived to provide future generations of cattle. I thought about the letter for a few weeks, and then in August, 2001, I sent a brief note thanking him for letting me know there were still some descendants of the original small herd we'd taken out there in 1965.

He responded shortly after, this time a properly addressed envelope, and described his interest as ' mostly curious' and just wanted to know more about the ranch story, since he was raised on a ranch. He would be working for a seafood plant there for the next six months and wanted to know more about Akutan.

As I felt more comfortable revealing the various events that took place on Akutan in the sixties, Doug started referring to me as the 'cow woman' when conversing with his family and friends, hence the title. As I became immersed in events that took place back then, my letters became quite lengthy and frequent. He responded with a fascination that encouraged me to continue telling him my story. Besides our ranch experiences, I described a village and a people that I interacted with between 1965 and 1970. He bluntly responded that the place I described no longer existed. I was stunned to discover that the new Akutan has little resemblance to the village I knew. To me, the old Akutan was the Shangri- La of the Aleutians. I am thankful that it existed when I was there.

Several years ago, I gathered my letters and notes and began this book, which may not have come about if it weren't for Doug Dodd's curiosity on how the cows came to be there and his persistence in the search for the answer. Thus, my story, along with the cows, is the remaining legacy of the ranch that Charlie Brown, Hans Radtke, and I started in 1965, and the often unpredictable adventures our family experienced during our five years on Akutan.

As a side note, after four months of corresponding, Doug proposed to me and I accepted, though we still hadn't met. We were married in June, 2002. Afterward, he encouraged me to put all my writings in a book, as I had made copies of my letters to him. Now that my story is completed, I am grateful to him for his help and encouragement. I also feel gratitude toward those cows. Without them, I wouldn't have met my husband.

Chapter

1

Bound for Akutan

A heavily laden seventy-five year old wooden freighter, the *MV Robert Eugene,* set sail from Seattle, Washington on a two thousand mile journey to the Aleutian Islands in mid-June, 1965. Noted for their frequent storms with powerful winds sometimes registering over one hundred miles an hour, the Aleutians hold the well-deserved title, Birthplace of Storms. Three novice ranchers—my husband Charlie Brown, our bachelor partner Hans Radtke, and I—accompanied by our two children, eight-year-old Becky and five year old Malcolm, had hired the boat.

We were transporting almost five hundred farm animals to the neighboring islands of Akun and Akutan, near the upper end of the chain of islands that curves far to the west toward Japan—between the North Pacific and the Bering Sea. This isolated location would be home for four hundred Columbia sheep, heavy with winter wool, fifteen full-grown Hereford heifers, one young curly faced pedigreed bull, six goats, two horses, a few laying hens and a rooster.

The animals, in multiple pens three tiers deep, filled the ninety-five foot craft from the depths of its deep hold to just under the long deck. They took up most of the space down below; so much of the cargo, such as bags of feed, bales of hay, and building materials, along with all of our earthly possessions, was piled on the narrow decks and covered with tarps, then lashed down with ropes and bungee cords, leaving minimal room for maneuvering through the outside walkway.

The remaining occupants included the skipper, slim, blonde, middle-aged Carl Flory, who had navigated those dangerous waters for many years operating tugboats that pulled barges from Washington to islands in the Chain, so he was the ideal choice. His first mate, Jack Graham—tall, slender and young—had assisted Carl on the *Robert Eugene* the previous year when the boat owners, Rufus and Alice Choate, brought their own livestock to Unalaska Island, forty miles from Akutan Island, having sold their Montana ranch and bought the boat to transport their animals to their leased grazing land on that island.

The Choates and their three children, one young teen boy and two grown children, a daughter and a son, were also aboard as they were taking additional supplies and stock to their one year old ranch, which added to the boat load but subtracted from the cost of our lease.

Rufus Choate had lined us up with a Montana stock buyer to obtain our animals and have them trucked to Washington, to begin the next leg of their journey to their new home. Rufus had helped Charlie and Hans make out an order of everything he thought they might need, as he had raised sheep for many years. None of us had been around sheep; we relied heavily on what information Rufus shared with us, though his own knowledge of sheep ranching in the Aleutians was limited.

Charlie and I had moved to Alaska in 1958 from Silver City, New Mexico to teach at Seward High School. After we taught that first year, we both left teaching for better paying jobs, Charlie with Standard Oil in Seward and I with Seward General Hospital as Director of Nurses, since I was also a Registered Nurse.

In 1961 his employer transferred him to Dutch Harbor, in the Aleutians, to work at their facility, so I quit my job and our two children and I followed him. Among the many boats that came to that dock were some that were loaded with wool from the neighboring islands, on their way to the Washington market. Charlie spoke fondly of growing up on his father's

Hans is repainting the name on the seventy-five year old stock boat, in May, 1965, while it is docked in Seattle awaiting the delivery of the truckloads of animals from Montana.

June, 1965, one of the trucks transporting our livestock from Montana, sits on the Seattle dock. We had a stock buyer purchase all of our animals and arrange the shipping to Seattle. On a scale of 1 to 10, I knew zero about ranching and I think Charlie and Hans overestimated their location on that scale.

remote Hereford ranch, high in the New Mexico Mountains, above the town of Alamogordo. He wanted to look into sheep ranching as the animals seemed to do well in the moderate, damp climate, and he said it would be a healthy environment for our two children. I had an adventurous nature so I thought it was a great idea. The federal Bureau of Land Management was making a large selection of land available for grazing leases, homesteads, and five-acre home sites, including some land on islands in the Aleutians.

We had met Hans in 1963 when Standard Oil sent him and another painter to Dutch Harbor to paint five houses leased from the Navy. At twenty-eight, he had been in this country several years, having emigrated from Germany. His accent was heavy, but his English was good so he was easy to understand, and he liked to practice his adopted language. During the month he was at Dutch a deep friendship began among the three of us as we sat around in the evenings and got better acquainted. We talked about our ranch plans and learned that Hans had already had similar thoughts, even though he wasn't a U.S. citizen yet. We shared our dream of someday having a ranch but realistically knew we had neither the money nor enough information about how to go about the lease procedure. Isolation has its drawbacks. But with Hans genuinely interested, we felt there was a real possibility it could happen if we joined forces. Back in Anchorage, where he lived when not out on jobs, Hans said he would contact BLM and find out what lease land was available in the Chain and get forms for us so we could begin making our plans. Hans was a bachelor, so with no ties he was free to pull up stakes.

The three of us had some savings, but now we had a goal, so we set aside even more of our paychecks, in order to prepare for the biggest expenditure of our lives. We also applied for and obtained an agriculture loan to help finance our venture. Charlie quit his job when the ranch partnership was officially formed in late 1964. As a result of these preparations, the last week in June, 1965, found our family on a loaded stock boat making the two thousand mile voyage to the Aleutians.

There were enough of us on board so that a feeding and watering routine could be worked out with Hans, Charlie, the two older Choate children and me. We used the slats on the sides of the wooden sheep pens as ladders

Hans is looking up from a pen on the *Robert Eugene* with Charlie behind him as they take water buckets down to all the animals. My job was taking hay down to the pens.

when we went down into them. They had low ceilings since they were three deep down in the hold and the animals didn't stand very tall. At just over five feet, I had to bend my head when I was in there hauling water and hay. The cows and horses had more headroom so Hans, at six feet ,and the older Choate son, also quite tall, took care of them and also helped the rest of us with the massive sheep flock. We were all on a schedule of four hours on and four off around the clock, though there wasn't always four hours of work to do each time.

The work was hard and tiring but seemed to go smoothly. We had esti-mated that the trip shouldn't take much over a week if all went well. Unfortunately, not enough consideration had been given to the unpredict-able Aleutian storm pattern.

We enjoyed good weather from Seattle to Kodiak with mostly rolling waves that seemed to rock the boat like a giant cradle. The heavy load was riding well without any needed adjustments, and no real complaints from the animal kingdom except when they were hungry. The boat was five or six days out of Seattle when we pulled into the Kodiak dock and were met by a rancher who loaned the Choates a pregnant Australian sheep dog. They were to keep the litter, but would give us two, and then return the female after her pups were weaned. We stopped there for about six hours that night and it felt good to get some rest while my bunk wasn't rocking back and forth. Cradles are for babies.

The seas were smooth as we took off early the next morning with only a cool breeze brushing my face while I stood on deck, staring at the bright green hills as they went gliding by. Because of the live cargo, Carl elected to take his chances with the open waters, with no visible land in site, rather than take the shortcut through the often-treacherous narrow passage, Shelikof Straight. With its frequent storms and boiling seas, the Straight, which ran between mainland Alaska and Kodiak Island, held the infamous reputation of being the graveyard for many unfortunate vessels. Bypassing it in favor of the unprotected waters seemed a good choice, till Carl rounded the south end of Kodiak Island. With land no longer in sight, a churning mass of ominous dark clouds appeared and began to overtake the blue sky.

The balmy breezes we'd experienced as we sailed out of Kodiak rapidly changed to strong winds, and then escalated to gale-force strength, as the blackened skies suddenly poured out torrential rains. Too far from shelter, we could not turn back. We were caught in the middle of the storm and had only one option: weather it out. The winds continued to gain momentum, approaching sixty-five knots—almost seventy-five miles an hour—tossing the MV Robert Eugene about with alarming force, a change so sudden it caught us unprepared. Spray crashed over the bow as the old wooden boat rose high in the air, reaching a dangerously steep angle, on the crest of thirty-to-forty foot waves.

I told Becky and Malcolm to remain in the cabin below deck; then I left to help with the animals, following the feeding and watering routine that we had worked out earlier. But when I went up topside I found it hard to push forward against the powerful winds as the narrow deck tilted wildly, pitching and rolling, as rain mixed with salt spray stung my face like cold

Docked in Seward, June of '65, the first stop in five days, since leaving Seattle, Charlie is standing partly on the dock and partly on the *Robert Eugene*.

needles. I lurched along, grabbing for handholds on the tilting rail to steady myself and keep from getting swept overboard.

Making my way to the hold, I saw Charlie and Hans in bright yellow raingear, lashing the deck cargo down tighter while they, too, struggled against the violent rising and plunging of the boat. Suddenly, despite their efforts, some of the bales of hay and bags of feed became dislodged as I watched, and slid over the side into the dark churning waters of the Pacific. The crashing waves and roaring wind were so loud I didn't hear them hit the black undulating mass; they were just swallowed up.

Finally reaching the hold, I heard the cows bellowing in their fear and misery above the din of the raging storm as they were flung about. In the sheep pen I was overwhelmed by the stench of ammonia, burning my eyes and settling in my nostrils. But cleaning the pens was not an option; I could barely keep my footing on planking that tilted and pitched like the floor of an amusement park funhouse. The terrified ewes, eyes bulging wildly from their sockets, made pitiful noises as though begging me to stop their stable from moving. I worked fast, throwing hay as far away from myself as I possibly could, to keep them from blocking my escape route. Still some of the sheep crowded around me several times, preventing me from reaching the ladder. I feared I would be trampled to death, unable to move as they pressed their thick bodies against me. I yelled for Hans in a panicky voice, as he was working in an adjoining pen. He came to my rescue each time, tossing hay away from me to divert the animals in a different direction while I moved fast toward the ladder.

After my shift ended, I returned exhausted to my bunk for rest, but none was to be had. I lay there in my drenched clothes, clinging to the ladder mounted on the side of the bunk, to avoid being thrown onto the floor as the force of the mammoth waves sent the boat pitching to one side, throwing everything into chaos, until, with a violent heave, she would right herself just as rapidly. But before any order could be restored, she'd lunge onto her other side, pausing only momentarily, before repeating the endless cycle, as I was thrown first into the wall on my right, then the ladder on my left, in that nonstop pattern. From my bunk, I observed the old wooden hull separate and come together making rhythmic creaking sounds, as if the ship had lungs.

It seemed only minutes later before my turn came again to help with the feeding and watering.

Battered and bruised from the tossing in my bunk, my body chilled under waterlogged work clothes, I climbed back out on deck and made my way along the narrow slick path toward the ladder to the pens. I sometimes feared I could be swept overboard, as I saw the bow plunge deep into the black waves with a thunderous crash, momentarily disappearing into the dark depths, only to rise again, breaking through with a deafening roar as it soared high into the air, huge blinding sheets of water pouring off her.

Carl, at the helm, fought to quarter the monstrous waves and avoid the more dangerous troughs that would render us more vulnerable to capsizing. For thirty-six hours, he and Jack remained in the wheelhouse, their faces taut with concentration, spelling each other as they navigated the mighty storm.

The ex-fireboat, *Robert Eugene*, pulled into Akutan on July 1, 1965, sitting low in the water with a virtual farm on board along with all the worldly possessions of five people, plus large quantities of building material and animal feed.

Then there came a remarkable change: the rolling seas had rapidly turned into gentle waves and when I came up from the hold the *Robert Eugene* was almost gliding, like a distance runner taking a victory lap.

To bring us safely through, we'd depended on the skilled seamanship of the skipper and his first mate, whose bravery and endurance as experienced sailors had saved our lives. To us, they were heroes.

Blue skies broke through clouds, along with rays of sunlight, the first we'd seen in several days. With the seas finally calm, we began to survey the damage. It had been impossible to prepare food all those many hours, just barely able to keep our footing. Crackers had been our main source of nourishment, washed down with endless amounts of coffee. Alice and I found a wreck in the galley as broken glass, grape jam, catsup, and other ruined provisions sloshed in a tide across the floor.

The lost supplies amounted to nothing compared with the heartbreaking loss in the pens when Charlie, Hans, and the Choates' older son pulled out fifteen dead sheep from the hold, crushed and trampled in the severe rolling. The carcasses were dropped into the sea, their limp bodies a grim reminder of the panic I'd felt down in the pens, fearing a similar fate in their midst.

Chapter

2

Tragic Welcome

On July 1, 1965, on a sunny afternoon, we sailed smoothly into Akutan Bay. I stood at the bow with Becky and Malcolm next to me, all three of us smiling in anticipation of our new home. I saw a mix of about twenty houses and small cottages clustered near the beach; some were gray weathered wood, others painted white. Steep green hills encircled the bay like a giant horseshoe, emphasizing the isolation of the Aleut inhabitants. Akutan Island was one of many that dot the Aleutian Chain, with most of them either uninhabited or sparsely settled.

The BLM had told us there were ninety inhabitants in that village as of the latest census. Except for the village there were no other inhabitants on the island, so there was lots of grazing land. About eight or ten men, women, and children were standing along the beach as we dropped anchor offshore and I wondered if they were just curious about the intrusion or were there to greet us. We were too far off shore to make out expressions.

I'd seen pictures of Akutan that Charlie and Hans brought back from their initial visit but this was my first glimpse of the place I had chosen to raise my family. It was a long way from Overland Park, Kansas where I was raised, just outside Kansas City, Missouri. I could barely control my smile as I felt that feeling that a person gets in anticipation of something wonderful about to be experienced. I imagined a carefree peaceful lifestyle, my vision of life in a remote area enjoying the simple life of a rancher's wife. It would soon become apparent that a little research and 'ranch wife interviewing' could have been both helpful and detrimental; that is, I might have forgone this experience. I'm glad that opportunity hadn't presented itself.

We had just dropped anchor, when a skiff shot out from shore heading full throttle toward us. I assumed it was a welcoming party, though I could make out only two men in the boat. One was on his feet, shouting, and waving his arms. The engine dropped to idle, as the small boat approached the *Robert Eugene* and pulled alongside. I leaned over the rail to better hear what I thought must be his excited words of greeting.

Over the thrum of the engines, I heard him holler, "We need a nurse! We need Mrs. Brown! A baby is very ill!"

My being an RN was one of the reasons the villagers had been in accord with the Bureau of Land Management in granting us a grazing lease bordering on a Native Reserve. Most of the small Alaskan Native villages had a local person who was sent to Anchorage and trained to be a medical aide, though they were limited in what they could do, just as I was in my own capacity, but since they could provide some medical help I hadn't planned to do any nursing, much less be greeted with an emergency. I felt something must be very seriously wrong or they wouldn't have come for me. I turned to Charlie and said, "I better go. Keep an eye on Becky and Malcolm. I'll get with you in the village later."

I climbed over the side of the freighter, high above the water, and let myself down on the slightly swaying rope ladder, into the waiting skiff.

Once I was aboard and seated the skiff sped off for the distant shore. I clung tightly to the side, braced against the wind and salt spray. As soon as the boat hit the shore and ran up the short beach, the two men and I leapt out.

The man who ran the boat tied it up, and the other one, the one who had called out to me, led me on the short walk along the worn wooden boardwalk that connected the small houses. The people from the beach followed us mutely, and stopped outside the house we entered.

This is Akutan village as it looked between 1965-1970. The houses were built close to the beach and fairly near one another. A wooden boardwalk connected all the houses. The well-maintained Russian Orthodox Church is at the end of the village, on the far left.

I stood in the doorway, breathless from the fast pace to that house. I observed seven or eight people sitting or standing silently in the small front room. No one offered me a greeting or introduced themselves, but I noted expressions of sadness on their faces, not unfriendliness. Many of them were looking downcast. I felt awkward in that somber atmosphere. I also sensed that something was terribly wrong.

My guide, in his forties and of medium height, told me his name was Steve. He led me to an adjoining room where a young woman held a tiny infant, three weeks old. She stood near a baby crib where her other child, perhaps one or two years old, languished. Steve whispered to me that the little girl in the crib had become very ill a few days ago and was getting worse. Her eyes were now rolled back, only jaundiced slits showing and her skin was an unnatural yellowish color. Short, infrequent gasps were just enough to signify a sign of life. She didn't have a diaper on, but was lying on a white cloth stained with a thin greenish liquid. A tiny line of yellowish crust ran down from the corner of her mouth. It didn't take a medical professional to conclude that the toddler was critically ill. I felt helpless, knowing what needed to be done for both of the children if facilities were available, frustrated that we were so far from medical help. In a case of severe vomiting and diarrhea a doctor usually starts intravenous fluid to counteract the dehydration and electrolyte imbalance. A lab would run a culture to check for the cause of the illness and proper medication would be given to treat it. All that would have been started before this toddler had reached this final stage.

"Does your village have a medical aide?" I glanced at Steve.

"She's in Anchorage right now." Steve turned to the woman. "This is Mrs. Brown from the stock boat that just came in. She's a nurse."

The mother lifted dark teary eyes toward me. I asked her what had happened. In a faint whisper, she said her daughter had been having severe diarrhea and vomiting for several days, then lapsed into unconsciousness that morning. It was now late afternoon.

I asked Steve, "What medical supplies are available?"

He replied, "Just basic first aid type items such as bandages and aspirin."

"Has the Navy Base at Kodiak been notified for possible evacuation?"

Steve said no, so I asked if someone would get on a marine radio and begin what was often a long and tedious process of trying to get through. I had already experienced this during my years in Dutch Harbor. He said his wife could do it.

The nearest medical facility was on Kodiak Island, an hour and a half by seaplane, but that time frame was misleading. The planes were dependent on daylight and passably calm water; no airstrip existed here. To complicate a rescue operation further, the people of Akutan had no direct communication with Kodiak. The townspeople relied on a cumbersome relay process to get messages to the Navy Base. Using a marine radio, they had to raise the radio operator at Scotch Cap, a small military facility about fifty miles east of Akutan Village that relayed messages to Kodiak. But if Scotch Cap wasn't listening on the same frequency, hours could pass before a response came from this intermediary.

Steve left the house to make arrangements for the emergency transmission.

I turned my attention to the infant that the mother had been holding the whole time as it sucked on a bottle that contained a white liquid, probably baby formula. I saw her hold him over her arm, its face turned toward the floor as he vomited small amounts of curdled milk. Then she turned the baby toward her. He sucked a few times on the baby bottle she offered; then regurgitated again.

I reached for the infant. "Here, let me hold him. He shouldn't drink any more for now. Why don't you lie down? I'll do what I can till the Navy arrives."

She handed me the tiny bundle. Then the woman, near collapse, lay down on the narrow bed against the wall. She said her husband had just left for fishing, so relatives had tried to help but she couldn't rest, watching her daughter's condition rapidly worsen, and her baby boy then begin to sicken.

I felt there was little I could do for her daughter, and from my experience in pediatrics, it appeared the little girl would not survive much longer. I held the newborn and waited for news of a rescue.

A short middle-aged man with a sad expression stood in the doorway. He said he was the young woman's father. He thanked me for being there with his gravely ill grandchildren. His voice was very soft as he had already summed up the gravity of the situation. I knew his daughter was going to need him. I was glad he was there.

Soon the little girl let out short, occasional gasping sounds; I was sure they were her last breaths. I handed the baby to a gray-haired woman who had identified herself earlier as the mother-in-law and, lifting the small child from the crib, I placed her on the single bed by her crying mother to hold those last moments. After her daughter was gone, the mother rose and stood with her father's arm around her, numb and stricken.

Word went out to the front room where a handful of relatives and friends sat and stood, but I heard no wails of lament, only whispers, expressions of grief and sorrow on their downcast faces. The woman's father approached, thanking me, saying I'd always be welcome there. I appreciated his words but my work wasn't finished. I still had a gravely ill infant to care for till help arrived.

The news from the marine radio operator wasn't good. She had reached Scotch Cap and requested assistance but had cancelled it when she'd heard the child had died.

I told her, "The newborn is very ill with the same symptoms and needs to be evacuated."

She got back on the radio. But almost five hours would pass before she'd get through to Scotch Cap again. By the time the second call was picked up, it would be too late in the evening to begin the rescue flight.

Back at the house where so much tragedy was playing out, two men were making a small wooden coffin in the front yard out of some scrap lumber. In the children's room, the grieving mother sat on the bed holding the baby while two women attended to the dead child, wrapping her in a blanket. One of them turned to me and said they would prepare the little girl for burial elsewhere.

I remained in the house the entire night, tending the weakened, dehydrated baby. His mother slept for short intervals. She was exhausted from caring for the two children the past few days but through grief at her loss she didn't want the tiny baby out of her sight for long. He was mostly quiet throughout the evening and night, though sometimes he made a faint weak cry. He had stopped vomiting so I gave him small sips of water occasionally and could only hope that help would arrive in time. Others held him from time to time and I got some rest, taking catnaps in a chair. A few men and women kept an all-night vigil and spoke in hushed tones with each other in the front room. I lost all track of time but sometimes someone would come in to ask about the baby's condition. Gradually, they conversed with me a little and introduced themselves, though I was very tired and had to try and stay focused on the infant.

One of the women came to me and said softly, "I brought you some tea and a sandwich. Can I get you anything else?" I hadn't thought about eating, I was so caught up in the event at hand. Now I did feel hungry and was grateful for the woman's thoughtfulness.

"Thank you, this'll be fine," I replied.

It had been hours since I'd seen my family and although I could see from the window that the *Robert Eugene* was still anchored off shore, I didn't ask what might be happening out in the bay.

Just after dawn the next morning I heard the roar of a plane's engines. A child dashed into the house and told us the Navy plane was coming in. Outside a seaplane was landing in the bay near the village, a Grumman HU-16 rescue amphibian, too big to taxi onto the narrow beach. One of the men readied his skiff while the baby's grandmother bundled the infant in blankets and headed for the boat. She already had a small suitcase packed and someone carried it for her. The young mother stayed behind as she wanted to remain in the village for her daughter's funeral.

The Grumman, called the Albatross, rose, stirring up a huge plume of spray, leaving a long wake in the bay, a comforting sight to those of us on the shore, thankful that the baby had survived the night.

I would learn later that the baby was taken to the Alaska Native Hospital, referred to as ANS, and was treated for salmonella poisoning, which is an extremely serious condition, even in the best of circumstances. Thankfully, he returned to Akutan, a healthy infant some weeks later.

Once the plane departed, a man approached me on the beach and said, "I'll take you to a cabin your husband had arranged to rent. It belongs to a man we call Uncle Paul. He's a bachelor and is in ANS with terminal cancer."

The little dwelling—which I would hear was always referred to as Uncle Paul's cabin—was so close to the beach that the windows facing the bay had dried on salt spray from wind-driven waves. Only a small patch of ground separated it from the low bank. The exterior was weathered gray wood with some remnants of white paint that hadn't completely been worn away by the frequent storms. I wondered how five people could be fitted in there, not to mention our boxes. But as no other accommodations were available, I was grateful for any shelter. With much settling in to do, I knew it would be quite a while before Charlie and Hans could put up our own cabin.

Through the front door—its only door—I entered a small kitchen. A few men and women stood around talking. Becky and Malcolm ran to me; I bent down and wrapped my arms around them. The recent loss I'd witnessed made me cling to my own children, selfishly thankful for their very aliveness.

Charlie was there and came up to me. "We heard what happened. I bet you're tired but can I show you around now?"

"I'm about to fall asleep standing up. I'm exhausted. Everything you want to tell me or show me is going to have to wait. Just show me where the bed is." He showed me to a small bedroom where I collapsed on the bed in clothes I had worn for more than twenty-four hours, including my filthy jacket. I drifted off inhaling a potpourri of seawater, hay, and the musk of animals.

3

New Surroundings

After a few hours of sleep, I was ready to get up and explore Uncle Paul's cabin. I stood in the bedroom doorway and saw a couple of men and children standing in the tiny kitchen watching, while several others helped Charlie and Hans carry in our many boxes. I didn't notice any women, and thought some must be with the bereaved mother who had just lost one of her two children the day before and saw the other one leave on the Albatross that morning. I could see Becky and Malcolm out the kitchen window with several other children, smiling and talking. They looked happy. That lifted my spirits and I felt better. So much had happened in such a short time.

Since yesterday afternoon my whole focus had been on those two sick infants. My brain had shut out everything except the emergency. Normally a shy person, somehow I had been able to ignore the cluster of silent people, the unfamiliar surroundings in the house. I had not even considered my unkempt appearance, though I had come straight from foul-smelling stock pens that morning. My tangled windblown hair and spray-streaked face from the fast boat ride would normally have embarrassed me, but my concentration had been on the children.

Now at last, the reality of my arrival in Akutan set in. What a startling appearance I must have made, not the grand entrance I had envisioned. I wondered what must have gone through the villagers' minds when they saw me. How could they have placed so much confidence in me when I walked into that sick room? I could have spared myself that concern. As I came to know the people better, I realized their focus had probably been on the unfolding tragedy.

As I stood there taking everything in, I thought, "I'm here. I'm finally here." At last I could savor the excitement of the beginning of our Akutan adventure, which had only been a dream just a few years before. Tired as I was, I was happy to be there.

When Charlie saw that I was finally awake he stopped what he was doing and said, "Now that you're up, I'll take you on a tour, though I think you can see most of it from where you're standing." He had a little smile on his face, having the unique ability to see some humor in most situations, quite different from my more serious perception of things. However, he was not joking.

The bedroom I had just left was one of two, and only a little bigger than the boat cabin I'd just left. The wall-to-wall double bed was accessible only from the floor space at its foot. A small dresser with an attached mirror took up about a third of the remaining aisle. The 'closet' was a board with large nails pounded part way in. That worked well as I wouldn't have wanted an enclosed closet taking up any more of the space.

The other bedroom, Hans' room, about the same size as ours, had only a single metal cot with a flat metal spring and an almost flat blue and white canvas-ticking mattress. He placed some of his personal belongings under it since his room didn't have a dresser. His boxes were right up to the flat springs, so it didn't sag as some do when a six-foot, two hundred twenty pound man lies on it. With only the one piece of furniture, his room provided more floor space, so we stored our belongings there, stacked from floor to ceiling and several boxes deep. We had planned this as a permanent move for our family and Hans, so we'd brought everything that we hadn't given away or sold. Hans could barely get into his room so he was no better off than we were with the wall-to-wall bed.

Since the Choates were anxious to get back to their ranch on Unalaska, we had to unload all our gear and the animals as soon as possible.

A room that seemed the size of a postage stamp, was between the kitchen and our bedroom, and was referred to as the sitting room. It had a card table and two wood chairs, with not much floor space left over. It served as the dining area; the narrow kitchen didn't provide enough space for a table of any size. Becky and Malcolm claimed it as their bedroom at night when they unrolled their sleeping bags.

The kitchen's only appliance was an oil stove, used for cooking and heating. Later, I learned all the villagers had them in their homes—partly because of the absence of utilities, such as wood, coal, and AC power—partly because of its wonderful versatility. It provided constant heat year round, which made the often-damp summers more comfortable and stormy chilly winters more tolerable. Best of all it was wonderful to cook on. I quickly learned how to adjust the carburetor on the side of the stove to control the heat for frying, boiling, and baking, or just keeping the big silver teakettle warm.

The rest of the kitchen consisted of a worn linoleum-covered counter with a small white sink that featured a single cold-water faucet. The window above it looked out on the beach, a few yards away. There were also two wooden chairs, one next to the stove, conveniently placed for people to warm themselves when coming in. The other chair was next to the door that opened to the outside.

Off the small narrow kitchen was a room the size of a large closet, which served as a sort of indoor outhouse since there was no running water, only a toilet and a bucket, and no basin, no shower. The toilet was flushed with water from the bucket, which was filled from the single tap in the kitchen sink.

The sewer was a pipe, which ran straight from the cabin to the beach, a common solution for isolated coastal villages back in the '60s. We were told to flush the toilet only at high tide but occasionally I observed remnants of toilet paper on the beach. Some people couldn't or didn't want to wait for the tide. The frequent storms cleaned the beaches and exchanged our trash for the more desirable debris they left behind, such as the clear Japanese glass balls in shades of green and blue, about the size of baseballs, plus lots of beautiful shells like the perfectly formed sea urchin shells. I wondered if beaches on the other side of the world were littered with our empty cans and worn out shoes. I'm sure the toilet paper had long since dissolved into unrecognizable particles.

The electricity to the cabin and the other homes was DC (direct current), which was used mainly for lights. Because it was low wattage, the lights were fairly dim, but brighter than our gas lanterns, plus the fuel for the lanterns was a bit expensive and not always easy to get.

The power was provided by a generator in a hillside creek at the edge of the village. Every house was charged five dollars a year for the electricity. Luke, a former village chief, acted as treasurer and used the money for any needed repairs and maintenance to the system. When more money was needed the families chipped in.

Shortly after our arrival, some people came to me asking for help with tax returns and various other papers they needed to fill out as the forms were sometimes hard to understand. So Luke said the five-dollar electricity fee was waived for our family, as a way of thanking me. I was happy I had some service I could contribute to the community.

Some people had small AC generators so they could occasionally use record players and other AC items. Tommy McGlashan and his wife, Irene, used theirs for their wringer washer, though there were gas-powered washers, also. The school and the house that had the marine radio each had large capacity AC generators that ran all the time. With more knowledge about Akutan we could have brought a small generator in place of the boxes with my dresses, high heels, and other useless space-consuming items. And so much for my hair dryer and waffle iron.

After Charlie showed me how the facilities worked, I just wanted to wash up and find some clean clothes. The teakettle was our source of hot water, so I poured some in a basin I found on Uncle Paul's shelf and carried it into the tiny bathroom, along with a change of clothes. I felt pretty good about the cabin in spite of its inconveniences. We managed with the cramped quarters on the boat, so we could handle this. And the cabin had the advantage of being stationary.

Charlie left with a couple of men from the village and took a skiff out to the boat to begin the long unloading process.

Becky, Malcolm and I remained at the cabin getting better acquainted with our neighbors and surroundings. Often men, women, and children dropped in, usually without knocking. They'd simply walk in and sit down, sometimes without saying anything. The first time I walked out of the bedroom and saw a woman sitting in a chair by the oil cook stove I was a bit startled and asked what she wanted. She replied, "Nothing." Then I realized she just came to visit, a practice I was unfamiliar with in the busy world I'd left behind. I offered tea, the common beverage there, and took the other chair. Mostly we made small talk and got to know each other better.

After that initial surprise, I got used to finding people in my kitchen, and learned a lesson in slowing down, something I'd never had time for in my other life. I had come from a faster paced environment, but I found this new experience relaxing and enjoyable. The visitors often brought food, sort of like housewarming gifts and perhaps their way of thanking me for helping with the sick children. I know we were a bit of a curiosity to their isolated village. Their lack of knocking, just walking in and sitting down to visit was one way of signifying that we were accepted by their small close-knit family.

I enjoyed the openness, and in a short time the men, women, and children who stopped by to see me became much more communicative. I developed friendships there that I seldom have experienced elsewhere. A locked door was very uncommon, sort of symbolic of a lack of trust or unfriendliness. I quickly got used to unlocked doors and enjoyed the comfort of trust. Sometimes I viewed the village as a vast house with open-air passages between some of the 'rooms.' Our little house was just another room in their house.

Though I had planned to make Akutan my permanent home, sight unseen, before I arrived I wondered if the village people would accept us, or consider our presence as invasive. I assumed that because they lived so separated from much of the rest of the world, they preferred the isolation, living in a subsistence manner similar to an earlier civilization.

From the first day of our arrival on their Reserve, that question was answered. We were received with obvious friendliness, just like new neighbors on the block, not treated differently because we weren't Aleuts. They made no distinctions about our different backgrounds. Future circumstances proved their feelings were genuine.

I saw very little of Charlie and Hans as they worked from morning till late evening hauling animals. I made sandwiches for them to take, mostly tuna or egg salad, as our food choices were somewhat limited till I had time to get better organized.

The *Robert Eugene* had to be offloaded quickly as the animals needed to get ashore. Everyone looked forward to ending the feeding and watering routine down in the foul-smelling pens, and the animals could start grazing on the abundance of natural wild grasses and be able to get some much needed exercise and fresh air. It was close to shearing time for the Choates, so they needed to get to Unalaska, and our own flock needed to be sheared once the guys got set up. Jack, the first mate, was experienced at shearing and planned to return to help Charlie and Hans after he was done on the Choate ranch.

Besides leasing roughly half of Akutan Island, we had leased all of the small-uninhabited neighboring island of Akun about six miles from the village, and separated from it by a narrow passage through often turbulent waters. The guys wanted the two islands so the sheep could roam and graze all over the smaller one, while the horses and cattle, plus our cabin, would be on Akutan at the head of the horseshoe-shaped bay, in close proximity to the village. It looked like a good plan on paper.

The unloading for Akun took many trips over several days hauling the Columbia sheep, a breed recommended by other ranchers in the Aleutians, whose experience had been that they did well in the damp climate of the islands. Their coloring is characteristically a solid off white, what I'd call dirty white, but we also had a few black sheep, which I thought was kind of special.

An opening in the hull of the *Robert Eugene* formed a ramp, which the sheep were sent down, into a large wooden skiff that the village used to offload bigger boats that brought in various supplies from time to time. The skiff's stern was wide and flat so it held about forty sheep plus two or three guys. It was slow going in that open boat as it was not powered, but was towed by a village skiff through the narrow passage to Akun, which had

Hans is unloading sheep from an opening on the side of the *Robert Eugene* and placing them in the village skiff, to be towed to Akun Island. Jack Graham in yellow rain gear is standing by to assist, along with helpers from the Akutan village.

Charlie, Hans and Jack Graham, plus about forty Columbia sheep. They look pretty good after their very long journey by truck from Montana to Seattle, then ten days by boat to Akutan, and now on their final journey to their new home on Akun Island.

strong rip tides sometimes. After unloading the sheep on shore, the skiff was brought back to the freighter for the next load.

During the process of sending the sheep down the ramp to the skiff two of them ended up with leg injuries from the rapid, somewhat steep descent with other animals pushing behind them, so Charlie brought them to the cabin in the evening and we made little homemade splints and wrapped strips of cloth around them. We kept the two sheep in a corner of the small kitchen for about a week till they seemed like they could get around okay. They became quite an attraction for the children who came to visit Becky and Malcolm. We had a petting zoo in our cabin!

After all the sheep were unloaded, they hauled enough of the building supplies to Akun to construct the shearing and storage shed. Jack and some of the village men who had not left for fishing were a big help with all the unloading and hauling.

When they were done, the *Robert Eugene* moved as close as possible to the head of the Akutan bay, though it was quite shallow for a long way out, so the cows and horses had to be transported from there to shallow water in the skiff. Throughout all the days of this difficult procedure, the usually misty or windy weather remained remarkably calm, a big break for the guys, and of course, for the animals. Even with good weather, it was slow and exhausting.

When the cows were put into shallow water they swam ashore, a somewhat unusual sight to see, one that some of the villagers who had gone there to watch remembered many years later. It was the first day of freedom for the cows in over three weeks, having endured a very long journey. The stock buyer in Montana, recommended by Rufus Choate, had purchased some very hardy heifers for that arduous trip as they all made it in good shape, having been trucked to Seattle, and then put into pens down in the belly of that old wooden boat. After ten miserable days at sea, they had to wait their turn to disembark, and with so many sheep, that created a few more days' delay for those sixteen cows. I'm sure they didn't realize their good fortune, that we only wanted them for breeding purposes, not eating. They behaved in such a calm, placid way I felt they must not worry much about anything. Once ashore, they banded together and immediately began grazing on the foot high wild grass. Slowly the herd ambled away from the beach, though never out of sight.

The head of the bay is flat for about three quarters of a mile along the beach and toward the steep hills, though swampy in parts, with lots of spongy moss covering some areas and several creeks running through it. Since I was not very familiar with cows I was a little surprised at how quickly they adapted to their new home environment.

The two horses, geldings, proved to be much smarter than cows. While they had put up with the inconveniences and discomfort and lack of exercise the same as all the other animals, their instincts told them they were destined to be workhorses if they stuck around. Once off the boat, unlike those placid Herefords, they took their freedom and ran with it at the first opportunity. When first taken ashore, a rope was placed around a leg and attached to a stake in the ground. After the unloading was completed, the guys removed the ropes and attempted to put bridles on. The horses took off.

High rugged hills completely surround that area. Yet in spite of their previous cramped living conditions, they had the strength and agility to outrun Charlie and Hans and head for the nearest hill, so high and steep it was almost a mountain. I never saw them again.

Occasionally Charlie and Hans spotted them when they made horse hunting expeditions to the other side of the high hill, but those two animals were too wild—or too smart—for the guys to get close enough to lasso them. They seemed to prefer the beach grass and riding out the severe storms with no sheltering trees, to oats and sugar cubes, an eventual stable. Over the years villagers told us of sightings while out duck hunting or hiking. But they were never able to get near them. As things turned out the horses were not really needed, and certainly not the two saddles and tack we had brought.

After all the stock and supplies were unloaded on the two islands the boat, her crew, and the Choate family headed for Unalaska forty miles away. As I watched the *M/V Robert Eugene* sail out of Akutan bay, sitting much higher in the water, I remembered how she had performed when, heavily loaded to the very depths of her creaking old hull, she had weathered that terrifying storm. If boats could receive medals for bravery, she deserved a 'Silver Star.' I didn't know that would be the last time I would see her.

That old boat had a unique history. Originally named the *Snoqualmie*, she was the first and only fireboat in Seattle in 1890, the year she was put into service. Then in 1909 the boat, considered worn out and unseaworthy, was replaced by a larger, steel-hulled vessel. But in 1910, the *Snoqualmie* got an overhaul, and was converted from coal-fired to oil-fired power. In '36 she was refitted to a freighter, and with her new makeover, she was given a new name; the *M\V Robert Eugene* was born.

Some years later I learned that in the early 1970's the former fireboat had an ironic end. Still in use into her eighties, that legendary old workhorse caught fire off Kodiak Island and sank. The *M/V Robert Eugene* defied the detractors that had branded her as unseaworthy so many years before. Her fiery demise was perhaps more fitting than being left to slowly rot in a boat graveyard.

Now it was time to adapt to ranch life. Charlie and Hans had their work cut out as the Aleutian summers were short, and the children and I had ours, just getting settled in to our new life.

4

First Summer

Before heading to Akun to begin building the shearing structure, Charlie spent half a day turning an empty weathered shed next to the cabin into a chicken house with roosts, nests and a small opening that entered a fenced off area. The Choates had brought along some Rhode Island Reds—a large breed known for being good layers- to take to their ranch. They sold five to us, four hens and an overprotective—actually hostile—rooster that I came to dislike intensely. Caring for them fell to me. It would become a real chicken blankety- blank job.

After Charlie and Hans left early the next morning for Akun to work on the shearing shed, I fed Becky and Malcolm breakfast and sent them outside to play. Then I began my first day of ranch duties, caring for the chickens. I assumed they'd be pretty happy in their new home, after almost two weeks of riding topside in cages on the boat. Armed with a scoop of chicken feed and a pitcher of water, I headed for the coop (its new name), about ten feet from our cabin door.

Both hands full, I naively entered and it was an eye-opener (closer) for me as the large brown rooster sprung straight up in the air, lunging at my face as if shot out of a cannon, talons, spurs and beak preceding his body.

Startled, I spilled some of the water while shielding my almost closed eyes with my arm, covered with the worn heavy boat jacket that could handle a few more rips and tears. I dashed back out the door, still clutching a can of feed and half a pitcher of water. This could not be a one-trip operation for me. I re-entered with one arm almost completely across my face, the feed scoop in the other hand. He attacked again, but this time he had lost the element of surprise, a key ingredient in Sun Tzu's ancient philosophy of war. I escaped with only minor hand scratches and slight rips. All the while the docile hens pecked away at their feed as if they were deaf, dumb and blind. I could sort of grasp why they might need a protector, and why that protector felt an instinctual obligation toward the hens and the eggs because I was there to steal their unborn babies. I still took the eggs. Then I had to go back and get the water.

Each time I left the coop I felt lucky to make my escape, not only with some eggs but also with both of my eyes intact. Of the five hundred animals we brought, that rooster was the only one that scared me. I always eased open their door and tried not to make a sound, but he could smell fear and instantly flew at my face with his built-in weapons.

Since the chickens could go out the little opening to the fenced run whenever they wanted to enjoy the damp breeze, I tried watching to see when that hated creature was in the yard and then sneak in. For a so-called domestic fowl with a head the size of a lemon, he had powerful hearing. Though I stealthily slid the door open just wide enough to squeeze in, he somehow sensed my presence and raced to that small opening like his tail feathers were on fire, and then burst into the coop ready for battle. I had been around hostile aggressive roosters before but not one that was a sociopath. I think attacking me was the highlight of his day.

Why was I stuck with these chickens? This was not my idea of being a sheep and cattle rancher. I hadn't given much thought to the mundane chores that accompany ranching. I was a city girl—sort of. I had to keep reminding myself that if we wanted fresh eggs someone had to care for the provider. It was do battle with that over-protective rooster or help shear three hundred eighty-five smelly sheep, after enduring a treacherous crossing to reach them, and I'm not a fan of rough water.

I devised a cardboard shield to protect my face, and juggled everything else with the other hand. Surprise, it worked. I just had to replace my scratched and shredded shield occasionally.

One day as I kept waiting to see my enemy out in the yard, it got later and later in the morning and the hens were doing more clucking than usual. I figured they were out of food and/or water by then and letting me know it. I got tired of waiting for the cock-of-the-walk so I carefully opened the shed and squeezed in, but no rooster jumped up at me. Instead—and let me say right now I'm innocent—he was lying stiff and staring in a corner. I didn't miss him; however, his harem apparently did and soon after his demise they began dropping off, one by one. I didn't know if they blamed me, but that was the end of our fresh eggs that summer.

The loss of the hens, while not as serious as the death of the fifteen sheep on the voyage, was not a good sign. As shoestring ranchers, we were devastated by what came next. On the morning of August first, exactly one month from the day we arrived, Charlie and Hans left for the head of the bay to check on the cows and work on the barn, so they told me they wouldn't be back till late. It was a warm sunny day, not all that common on the island, so they needed to get a lot of the construction done and they hadn't even started on our cabin. I was a neophyte at this farming/ranching business, but I'd heard that the barn comes before the house, so I just expected to wait my turn before I could move out of Uncle Paul's. Around noon I went to the small kitchen sink and happened to glance out the window and was startled when I saw the guys pull up on the beach in front of the cabin. I wasn't concerned; I just thought they came back for something, though I didn't know why both of them made the trip.

I went outside to meet them and noted they kept their heads down as they walked up the short bank.

Puzzled, I called, "What's up?"

Charlie looked at me with a grim expression, but didn't answer as they walked toward me.

"What's the matter?"

Charlie said, "Let's go inside."

I didn't like this. Something was wrong, but how bad could it be? I turned back to the cabin and they followed me in.

Once in the small kitchen, Charlie sank into a chair and said, "Bad news. We lost one of the animals."

"What happened? How did we lose it?" I thought of both the financial loss and the small herd now reduced by one.

"Sit down, Joan." Hans spoke in his usual blunt, matter-of-fact manner. He may have anticipated my reaction as well as Charlie, but he never wasted time with sugarcoating. Why should I sit? Charlie had already dealt the first blow, but I didn't argue with Hans, I sat in the one remaining kitchen chair.

In a gruff voice he said, "Ve lost da bull. Ve tink he broke his neck." His expression was solemn. He never minced words. He may have been upset because of our financial loss or because he was angry at the animal for some sort of stupidity on its part. As I came to know Hans better it had to be the latter. He didn't allow much slack to man or beast.

I was stunned. "The bull? Duke Pride?" I blurted in a rather loud tone. I was just starting to absorb the idea of losing a cow so early into our operation. Charlie knew me better than Hans and didn't want to be the one to tell me it was the bull. Though the sheep were our primary focus, we also hoped to build a quality herd by getting not just any bull, but a registered bull. Duke Pride held the distinction of being our most expensive farm animal. He held a pedigree from a Colorado ranch before he was brought up to Montana. Since Charlie grew up on a New Mexico Hereford cattle ranch, he was familiar with the breed and thought they should do well in the Aleutians.

"What happened?" I asked, feeling a little calmer, still unable to take in the full reality of the situation.

"We were almost to the head of the bay when we spotted a cow lying on its side, legs stretched out and head turned back in an unnatural way," Charlie said. "We knew something was wrong. As we headed toward the animal we saw a large clump of fresh dirt with high weeds near where it lay. Looked like it got too close to that overhang and it couldn't support the animal's weight. When we got close enough we saw that it was our bull. It was Duke." His voice dropped a decibel. He'd had time to take this all in on the way back to town, but I could tell he was hurting. "We ran the dory up the beach and he was dead for sure; probably broke his neck in the fall."

I felt sorrier for Charlie and Hans than Duke Pride. It was bad enough that we started out with so little funds to undertake such a huge operation. Our only sources of income were outside jobs and wool sales. A lot had been riding on that costly bull; however, clumsiness had not been bred out of DP's pedigree! He may have been the pride of Colorado, but he wasn't the pride of Akutan, losing his title after only one month.

"Ve gonna have to vait till spring and see if ve get any male calves, den it be another year before ve get any more, and maybe ve don't." Hans sounded a little discouraged, mixed with his anger. But unlike Charlie, he didn't internalize things; he'd get over it quickly and move on.

Charlie added, "You're right. It'll be many months before we can know what kind of legacy Duke left behind. Let's hope we get at least one male."

So much for our cattle empire. Ironically, over our remaining years on Akutan, we never lost another cow to falling. We should have got two bulls and forgot about the horses.

"That makes eighteen animals we've lost so far, plus a couple hundred dollars' worth of feed and supplies that went over the side. That's a significant chunk of our investment and we've barely got started. This is already costing more than we anticipated. Nothing's gone right so far." I heard a rare note of anger in Charlie's voice. "I hope we can at least get a good check for all that wool we sent off. We've got to get something out of all this."

"I know. The original plan for our main source of income was always going to be the sheep, not the cows. And with this terrain we don't really need the horses. Let's just wait to see how things work out with the sheep." I think I sounded pretty calm, but I didn't know how much longer I could hold back the tears. I just wanted them to leave.

"I'm beginning to wonder if this ranch wasn't a mistake. We dumped our life's savings into it. I quit a good job at Standard Oil—for this?" He sounded bitter and didn't look at me.

"It's only been a month. Let's just give it some time," I said as I wondered why they were still there.

"Charlie sat staring at the floor, as if he hadn't heard me. Then he blurted, "Maybe if things don't work out, the Choates will buy our stock, or maybe somebody else will buy what we have here."

Where did that come from? He had not confided that thought to me before, and for good reason. We would have had a pretty big argument. I wanted to be here. I wanted a place I could call home. I was enjoying the uniqueness of the village life and the warm acceptance I'd received from the people. I had come prepared to make this my home for the rest of my life; I thought Charlie had, too.

Before I could respond, Hans jumped in, and I could tell he had no such thoughts.

"Stop dat kind of talk, Charlie," Hans commanded. "It's only a bull. It's going to take more den dat to just give up. Ve got vork to do. Now, let's go." I had an ally; we were one-third equal partners.

He ushered Charlie out the door and they headed for the dory. Charlie picked the right partner, one who didn't allow setbacks to influence his decisions. At age thirty, Hans was five years younger but had lived a difficult life. He and Charlie had bonded like brothers so I thought he could snap Charlie out of that defeatist attitude.

Once they were on the beach I let it all out and buried my face in a pillow in the bedroom and had my private cry. I'd be okay once I got that over with. I reminded myself that Becky and Malcolm were my primary concerns. It would take more than one dead bull to uproot me. At the time I didn't place a lot of importance on the cows. In my own mind they were more like a sideline, just to round out the ranch. I couldn't know, thirty-six years later, the influence they would have on my life.

A few weeks later, we added two more animals, this time of the canine variety. Charlie went to the Choates at Unalaska on a fishing boat and picked up two female Australian Shepherd pups from the litter that had been born the day we pulled into Akutan and were now weaned. We named them Sugar and Malt, key ingredients in homebrew. I don't know which of the guys named the dogs, but they turned out to be inseparable, so I guess they were aptly named. They were identical in size and shape though their markings were distinctly different. Sugar had the traditional Australian Shepherd seal skin coloring, gray with black spots and a little bit of brown and white in a few places; Malt was a mix of brownish blonde.

Early on, Sugar seemed to react to any given situation first, with Malt following. Over the years Sugar demonstrated her superior abilities, which included responding to many words. On a lot of occasions she behaved as though she understood everything we said. Malt was also a very capable and obedient work dog, though passive, and didn't seem to have as good a grasp of the English language—sort of like a child that just gives you a blank look as if not understanding the question. Maybe Malt **was** the smarter dog!

When Charlie and Hans took the two pups to Akun to help with the herding of the almost four hundred scattered sheep, the dogs went right to work. Sugar led and Malt followed, both born to the job. They were fast learners and soon knew many commands. The only predators on the islands were red foxes, which we spotted occasionally wandering solo on the hillsides surrounding the bay. The only predators of the foxes were dogs, two in particular. Although Sugar was barely more than a pup and hadn't reached her adult weight of about thirty-five pounds, she was amazingly aggressive. Once a fox was spotted, Sugar and Malt took off at full gallop, Sugar in the lead. We never saw a fox outrun them. Once the dogs caught up, Sugar darted past the fleeing predator, and then turned on it, blocking its ability to go forward, while Malt remained directly behind it. Then Sugar lunged in, clamped her jaws on the back of the fox's neck and with a toss of her head, snapped its spine. They never once killed, threatened, or chased any of our animals, neither the original ones nor the ones we later added. They just didn't like foxes. Maybe there was something menacing about those creatures. Centuries before, they had been given the attribute of slyness but Sugar and Malt must have seen right through their stealthy behavior.

Late summer, the death of a villager somewhat affected us. I was in the cabin one Saturday afternoon when there was a knock at the door. The people usually walked right in so the knock seemed a bit formal. When I opened the door there were several villagers standing there.

"We came by to tell you we got word that Uncle Paul passed away in the Anchorage hospital."

It was no surprise, but I had wondered what would happen to this place after his death. I had known he was terminally ill, but I didn't know how long we could keep some of our things stored in the cabin and have the use of it when we needed it. With all the construction work that needed be done plus looking after so many animals, I anticipated a late start on our cabin. Back in '65 there weren't a lot of young men in that small village and the majority of them were gone on fishing boats, but a few that remained helped Charlie and Hans on Akun and the head of the bay. Still, I was concerned about a place for the children and me.

After the three entered the narrow space one man, the former village chief Luke Shelikoff, stepped forward. "Uncle Paul left a note here that says he wanted to leave his cabin to Anesia Kudrin."

As I mentioned earlier, she was the village health aide, and had also been very friendly to me, having invited me over for tea one morning to get better acquainted. Since Uncle Paul was a bachelor and lived alone, I thought she may have helped with some of his care.

"We need the paper. It's a little piece of note paper and we think he had it on the mirror in the bedroom."

The village was classified as an Alaska Native Reserve (not a reservation, though I never knew what the distinction was), but their homes were their own. The people visiting me knew about the paper and what it said. They just had to physically have it, I guess to prevent any future disputes about ownership. They were living in a place without lawyers, and in many ways I envied the simplicity of their lives. Why would they need lawyers when everyone was so trusting? In spite of our own setbacks I was happy to be a part of such a remarkable community.

Of course, I remembered the little piece of paper as it was unique in its size, content, and placement. When we moved into the cabin it had been emptied of all personal effects, exclusive of the few furnishings I mentioned earlier, except for a little piece of lined paper ripped from a pocketsize spiral tablet and stuck into the side of the dresser mirror's wood frame in our bedroom. It wasn't folded or in an envelope so I knew that it said in the event of his death he was leaving the cabin to Anesia. I handed it to one of my guests, who remarked that it was all they, the villagers, needed. Transfer of ownership was completed.

Anesia was already my friend, now she was our landlady. The next day she stopped by and told me we could keep renting the cabin as long as we needed it and the rent would remain the same, a very reasonable forty dollars a month. The guys would be glad to hear that as they still hadn't started work on our cabin, claiming more pressing ranch-related building projects needed to be completed.

The summer turned out to be quite a social one for me. The people had a fun custom of celebrating birthdays by inviting the entire village to 'tea', in groups of ten. The host family set out ten places at a table, then had children go house to house and invite ten people at a time for tea and their choice of desserts. The table was filled with a variety of cakes, pies, and cookies. I suppose it could be likened to birthday parties elsewhere, but one usually doesn't invite a whole community to help you celebrate!

My thirty-second birthday provided me with the chance to offer my own 'tea', to reciprocate for their unqualified acceptance and inclusion in their activities. Becky, though only eight, enjoyed cooking, especially baking, and helped me with the preparation of the various desserts. In spite of our cramped quarters and lack of seating, it felt like a very festive occasion, as they helped themselves to tea and a dessert and wished me happy birthday. It was the first time I felt I'd been able to repay them in a purely social way for their many kindnesses. Since most birthdays seemed to be celebrated in this manner, there were lots of teas and we looked forward to them because of the good food and the opportunity to become better acquainted with the people.

Another unforeseen event occurred in August, this one of a more positive nature. The Department of Education in Anchorage sent me a message over the marine radio that the superintendent for the schools in the Chain had just received word that the teacher scheduled to return to Akutan Grade School at the end of August had cancelled his contract. With school due to start in a month, they were in a time crunch for a position not easily filled on short notice.

While in Anchorage, before the trip to Akutan, we had checked with the Department of Education on the school system for our children. I mentioned that I held a current teaching certificate for the State of Alaska, in both secondary and elementary education, so I felt qualified to teach my children. I hadn't asked about a teaching position nor did I fill out an application, but someone in that office remembered that they had a licensed teacher right in the village.

When I got the call from Anchorage explaining the situation, I was offered the position of teacher-in-charge, a title given to head teachers in small schools. In this instance, though, I would be the only teacher, no other teachers, no teacher's aide, even. Basically, I would be in charge of myself!

The pitfalls and hard work involved in ranching had quickly tarnished my *'Little House on the Prairie'* vision of the new life I had so naively chosen. The teaching position provided a two-bedroom modern furnished apartment, much bigger than the cabin, attached to the one-room school. The door from the apartment opened directly into the classroom. The carpeted living room included a couch and an easy chair. The kids and Hans could share one of the bedrooms that came with bunks. Best of all, there was a city-type bathroom with water plumbed to the toilet. No more hauling buckets of water from the kitchen. The bathtub, one of only three in the village that year, could be filled with hot water right from the faucet, a luxury to me after having to heat water in a kettle on the stove for two months. No more spit baths or trips to the banya—the public steam bath house.

The school building had its own large generator that provided plenty of AC power, so I could use my appliances after all. The kitchen included the classic village oil stove, which again was also our source of heat. I was happy to see it now that I was spoiled for any other type of cooking range. There was also enough room in there for a table and enough chairs so we could all eat together, something the five of us liked to do as a family.

The government apparently spared no expense in bringing city comforts to the island, if only for the teachers they sent out—and I appreciated it as I was about to enter another unplanned chapter in my life. It remained to be seen if I could work with eight grades unassisted, but I was excited about the challenge. After our discouraging animal disasters, something good had finally come our way. Of course, I accepted.

Chapter

5

One Room Schoolhouse

We moved into the schoolhouse apartment a week before school started. We made lots of trips along the boardwalk as we hauled our mountain of boxes from Uncle Paul's tiny cabin with the help of some of the children. At last we could unpack most of our things.

The Enrollment that fall was twenty-five students, which was not an excessive amount in classrooms in those days, but what made it more challenging was the representation of all eight grades, with each of the grades having a variety of subjects to cover for their particular level. In addition, I was to be responsible for various forms and paperwork that a secretary would normally handle. With no lunchroom cook, I also had to find time to prepare their lunch or enlist some volunteer help, with the government surplus food sent to the school for that purpose. But I didn't have to chop wood and start up a wood stove before class, like some nineteenth century teachers. Progress was being made, though it was slow to reach the isolated Aleutian villages.

The day after we moved in, I explored the classroom half of the rectangular building. A stack of school mail had accumulated on the desk during the summer. I sat down and separated the material into piles to determine what required my immediate attention. The most important piece I saw was a packet that contained a very comprehensive order form listing everything from texts to pencils. My instructions were to take an inventory of what was already available, and then mark the items we would need for that school year, and then send it off on the next available flight.

I examined the textbooks on the shelves in the low bookcases that lined one long wall. Many had very old copyrights. One text that I picked up showed pictures of buses and trains, with captions stating, 'This is the main means of mass transportation in the United States.' I saw no pictures of airplanes, though they were a common means of transportation for getting in and out of Akutan in 1965. I checked that copyright- 1939. There were very few newer books. I called Charlie to come into the classroom.

"What's going on?"

"Look at these books. They're children's readers! Do you see those copyrights?" I exclaimed in amazement.

Checking the files for orders from other years I noted that a large portion of the allotted funds had not been used. Neither books nor supplies had been ordered the previous year. The catalog described lots of books that referred to airplanes, World War II, television, penicillin, and many other things that had been going on since 1939. I used up the entire book budget. I had a feeling it would be an exciting year for those children.

Then I went on to the P.E (physical education) inventory. I found only a few jump ropes and three or four balls. Some of the children told me P.E. and recess consisted of jumping rope and playing dodge ball, all in the classroom. They told me all twenty-five desks were pushed close together in the front of the room leaving a large area in the back half where they would play. The room itself was fairly large, around forty feet long, so space was not a problem.

Since the school was near the edge of town on semi-level weedy, and somewhat rocky uncared for terrain, built close to the hill that rose directly behind it, there wasn't a suitable place for playground equipment like swings, a basketball hoop, or a jungle gym, things we took for granted on school playgrounds in other communities. Besides the uneven ground, the often-inclement weather with the prevalent light mist and frequent strong winds, sometimes gale force, made indoor P.E. and recess more of a necessity.

In addition to the expected catalog offerings of jump ropes and balls, I was surprised to see a ping-pong table listed. The classroom was large enough to accommodate it, and the desks were easily moved around, so I thought, why not. The kids needed some variety. I put a check by it, though I wasn't sure it would make the final cut. The order was extensive and I needed to complete it before the next plane arrived.

Our mail service was provided by Reeve Aleutian Airway with a sea plane, the Grumman Goose, out of Cold Bay, about one hundred miles away. As there was no room for a landing strip, it pulled up on the short sandy beach at the opposite end of town from the schoolhouse. The villagers referred to it as The Goose. We were scheduled for two planes a month, but often three weeks passed between trips if the plane couldn't land.

Letters and forms from Juneau, Anchorage, and Washington, D.C. sometimes arrived weeks late and would be at least two or three weeks later reaching their final destination. Weather was always the controlling force. We would have to start classes with very limited supplies.

Juneau had to receive and process the orders from all the outlying schools before the state sent a large boat, the *North Star,* to deliver the school supplies to all the small villages with water access, which included the Aleutians. I hoped my order would reach them in time for the once a year boat delivery.

I eventually received confirmation from Juneau that did have it and the *North Star* was scheduled to arrive sometime in Akutan in October bringing our supplies, just when our stormier weather was also getting under way. But it had many stops to make first on its way to the scattered villages.

When school started the first week in September, I told the class they should be getting new textbooks and school supplies coming on the *North Star.* Then I talked to them about covering so many grades. "We have eight grades represented this year and lots of subjects to cover. I would like to make the day longer if you are in favor of it and if your parents agree."

I half expected some whining or arguing, not knowing how all of them felt about school in general, but when I asked for a show of hands about the extended day they were all in favor of the extra time, some even enthusiastic. There were no negative comments.

"We like being here, Mrs. Brown. There's more to do here," one of my fourth graders, Debby Pelkey, said. I think there was more to do in some of their homes, though, such as caring for preschool siblings and helping parents with their subsistence life style. But I was glad they enjoyed the school atmosphere

"Talk to your parents about it when you go home and I'll give you a note to explain it. I'll try to stop by and see some of your moms."

I had favorable reports from all the parents, so I outlined how the new schedule would work. School would start at eight A.M. and end at five P.M. They had an hour off for lunch and could go home if they liked, though the school would provide lunch if they chose to eat there.

"I'll need help with the lunches and snacks, so I'd appreciate it if some of you could lend a hand. Any volunteers?"

While the first and second graders were still a bit 'classroom' shy, all of the third through eighth graders waved their hands and shouted, "Me!" "Me!" "Me!" I was happy that I would have plenty of willing workers.

"I'll make a schedule and pair two of you to prepare the food and two to do the cleanup. In time you'll all get a chance to help. We will rotate students and duties, and when I get time I'll pitch in, too."

With the multiple grades and subjects, I knew I would need some assistance with the lower grades, so I asked the sixth, seventh, and eighth graders if they would be willing to tutor the younger ones when they had time available, especially with reading and math. Malcolm had the advantage of attending a Montessori kindergarten prior to our arrival in Akutan, which gave him a head start in learning his ABCs and counting, so he was able to assist his fellow first graders, Tommy and Lawrence. The older students never refused when asked to help other classmates, some of whom were their own brothers and sisters.

Often two or three children visited my two in the evenings, either playing or doing school work together; when Charlie and Hans were there some of the men would stop by. I often spent my evenings in the bedroom grading papers or working on the next day's lessons, so I didn't have much time for visiting during the week, but I enjoyed the homey atmosphere.

The school received a generous shipment of USDA surplus commodities for the lunches and snacks, but our menus were limited. There were big blocks of cheddar cheese, cases of Sailor Boy Pilot Bread (round crackers as large as saucers), large plastic buckets of honey and peanut butter, a one hundred pound gunny sack of pinto beans, and a similar one of rice. There were also many cases of Stark powdered milk, which arrived more as a solid block than powder, so hard it would not completely dissolve. At first I felt bad for the children because of the large hard lumps in their milk, so I was surprised that they preferred them. I often heard cheerful comments like, "I got more lumps than you did."

Our lunch menu never varied: beans three times a week, rice two times, always accompanied by Sailor Boy Pilot Bread with a slice of cheese and of course, the lumpy but popular Stark milk. Our two snacks a day were milk and the big round crackers covered with peanut butter and honey. Long after I left the island I continued to snack on Sailor Boy Pilot Bread with honey and peanut butter, a taste that grew on me. I never developed a taste for Stark powdered milk.

On the three days we had beans, I started them before class, setting the pot on the oil cook stove, which was always on anyway, but started the rice much later on the other two days. There was no budget for seasonings so I purchased salt for the beans, the only additive. That may sound a bit tasteless but I don't remember any complaints about the food, monotonous as it was. They had the option of going home for lunch, but they all chose to remain, talking and laughing all through lunch, using their desks as tables. Most of the children were either siblings or cousins and had grown up together on this isolated island, so they were used to spending a lot of time with each other. When lunch was over the two assigned to cleanup took over. I never heard grumbling from my kitchen, either from the cooks or the cleaners, mostly just giggling. I had already observed how well all the children seemed to enjoy each other's company.

The Akutan weather was often stormy, and some months were worse than others. October was one of them. So naturally in the semi-darkness of a late October afternoon, in the middle of a wild rainstorm, the *North Star* arrived in the bay. The lights of the big vessel distracted the students as they observed them through the rain-streaked wall of windows facing the bay.

Interrupting the class, Jimmy, my fifth grader, said loudly, "There's a big boat in the bay!"

"I think it's the *North Star!*" exclaimed Sam Stepetin, one of the seventh graders.

I had been mildly interested, thinking it was just another big vessel seeking shelter to ride out the storm. But Sam's outburst got my attention. At last, books and supplies! For over a month we'd dealt with antiquated material and only a few workbooks, which had made my work all the more challenging. I had previously taught at the Unalaska grade school, forty water miles away, and had an adequately stocked classroom with modern equipment and four teachers for fifty students. I didn't know how Akutan fell through the cracks, but I felt a surge of excitement that much of the problem would soon be resolved if that was the long-awaited *North Star.*

Peter Stepetin, who was Sam's older brother, along with three other siblings in my class, abruptly entered the classroom as water dripped down his face and off his rain gear, while he shoved the outside door closed behind him against the increasing wind.

"Mrs. Brown, we're going to need all your older boys out there to help us offload the *North Star!*"

The day had come! "Of course, they can go. Check with Charlie and Hans next door. They can run their dory out, too."

"I've already alerted them. I gotta get going now. Come on, boys."

Seven boys leaped to their feet and headed for the door, grabbing their jackets off the hooks. The remaining students left their desks and went to the four large rain-streaked windows to watch the skiffs head out, bouncing in the dark choppy waves. Offloading was a community activity and many men and boys assisted with their own boats. There was no longshoreman's pay or other compensation. The people always pitched in and did what needed to be done. Several men operated the wide village seine skiff used for subsistence fishing, the same one we had used to haul forty sheep at a time to Akun when we first arrived. All of the boats were open to the elements and the storm brought with it plenty of wind, almost guaranteeing a messy operation. I hadn't realized just how messy.

As the books and supplies were lightered ashore, wind-driven rain and waves splashed over boat bows onto the unprotected cardboard boxes in the open skiffs. Men and older boys wearing dripping yellow or gray rain gear and wet rubber boots hauled the soggy cases into the classroom where the students and I rapidly emptied them to lessen the damage. While I was working with the boxes, some of the students continued to monitor the operation from the windows.

"Mrs. Brown, some boxes fell overboard!" shouted Anna Stepetin, my third grader.

Oh no! I thought, and raced to the window. I saw boxes bouncing in the choppy waves as several boats attempted to retrieve them. I could only hope they weren't the long awaited textbooks, though I hoped whatever was out there could be recovered and at least partially salvaged. I found out later that a pallet had somehow spilled its load as it was offloaded in the mounting storm.

Surprisingly, only a few boxes were badly damaged. Those, the men carried in with their arms wrapped around the soggy mess to keep the contents from spilling.

Peter said, "I think we got them all and we tried to pick them up as fast as we could so they wouldn't get too soaked." Then he plunked down a pile of wet cardboard with tablets and colored paper sliding out of it. Thank goodness, not books, at least not in that one. Happily, when I went over everything, most of the books were in like-new condition. However, we ended up with a pretty good supply of wavy construction paper and water-spotted tablets.

Just as I was finishing up, several men hauled in a very large square but narrow box. The children's faces lit up when they saw what it was. A ping-pong table would be added to the jump ropes and rubber balls. I hadn't told them about it for fear they would be disappointed if they didn't get it. I sent a silent thank you to the Department of Education for honoring everything on my massive order.

The room filled with excited comments as the children observed the mounting pile of new books and generous supplies of paper, pencils, art materials and much more. After they had to make do for over a month with the odds and ends left from the previous year, not to mention the pre WWII text books—a few of which had some of their parents' names inside—they deserved the new material.

"Look!" exclaimed Anna, one of Pete's sisters, "Even new library books."

As Debbie and Becky started going through them like they were Christmas presents, I said, "Hey, girls, you can do that later. I can use some help here. We've got to get these wet boxes outside on the back porch. Becky, get a mop and wipe up some of the water that's all over the floor from everyone's wet boots."

After everything was opened and sorted, I sent the remaining students home with the promise that we would check out the new ping pong table the next day, plus everyone would get new text books to replace the worn outdated ones.

Everyone was on time the next morning waiting for school to open. Their excitement and enthusiasm showed in their smiling faces as we started the day. I was touched at how appreciative those children were about such ordinary school items as books and notebooks, items that students in many schools in the US took for granted as their due. Their attitude was later reflected in their enthusiasm to learn. It was a learning experience for me, too. Having so many grades and students was not all that difficult when a teacher has eager students, treating learning as a great adventure.

As I expected, the ping-pong table was a big hit. The children were fair about taking turns during our two recesses and lunch breaks. Sometimes I had evening visitors, though they didn't really come to visit me, but asked permission to go to the classroom and set up the table to play. I normally allowed it as no one abused the privilege.

Another diversion for the students was plane day. It was two or three weeks between planes and no amount of classroom discipline could keep them in their seats when one of the classmates would shout, "Goose!" above the roar of the plane's engines. I was startled when it first happened as I didn't realize the importance of the plane's arrival to the children. As well behaved as they were I felt like they had entered another time zone and I wasn't in it. With herd mentality, that word became the signal for them to stop in the middle of what they were doing, leap to their feet and head for the large windows. But just the sound of it was no guarantee the Goose could find a hole in the low cloud ceiling if the day were overcast, which was not uncommon. If the sound diminished, they returned to their desks with glum expressions. I, too, felt let down; discouraged because we didn't know when it would try again. Since the plane had other islands to service, we had lost our place in line.

Once the plane actually hit water they knew it would pull up on the beach and there was a mass exodus out the door, followed by a stampede down the boardwalk to the plane, actually only a short way. They watched as the plane pulled up on the beach, roaring and shedding water. Most of the town also turned out, as they, too, wanted to see who might have come in and what freight showed up, especially if they were expecting something. I quickly followed after the class as it was still school hours. When I caught up with them I went up to Robert, my eighth grader, and asked why everyone had run out. He told me they had always done that; the arrival of the plane was a big event for everyone. I became aware of that during the summer when lots of villagers, myself included (yes, I considered myself a villager too by now) headed for the beach when a plane pulled up, curious to see who came in and who was leaving.

I accepted the departure of the class without permission, since I understood the importance of the plane in their lives. I trailed them down the boardwalk each time, but after the Goose took off, I told the children that we had to get back to class. As I headed back to the schoolhouse, they fell in behind me like lemmings, though to a more pleasant experience than the ones in the fable. Plane days were special, but they weren't holidays and school wouldn't end till 5P.M. So that I wouldn't get behind in my lesson plan schedule, I explained to the class that those trips to the beach would count as one of their recess periods, and that it would have to be done in a more orderly fashion. We were only talking about two recesses a month.

Chapter

6

While I was Teaching

Charlie and Hans spent much of the first summer and fall on Akun Island where they built the shearing and storage shed, followed by the long tedious process of shearing three hundred eighty-five sheep, using clippers without electricity. Jack Graham, the former first mate from the *Robert Eugene,* was also a skilled sheep shearer and helped them, both with the shearing and the instructions, since this was a new venture for the guys. Also, some of the men from the village who had worked on the huge Nikolski sheep ranch in the past gave the guys a hand.

Because the Aleutian weather was notorious for going from a gentle breeze to high winds in minutes, there were times when they remained on Akun up to a week, depending on the severity of the storm. Sleeping bags and provisions were kept in the rough hastily built storage shed for such occasions.

Between Akun and Akutan is Akun Straight, a narrow stretch of water that is fed by the Bering Sea, and can be dangerous to traverse because of powerful riptides, water agitated by conflicting currents that go from flat calm to churning seas without warning. However, our dory could handle some very rough water as its design made it more seaworthy than a lot of conventional skiffs. Charlie respected those riptides and treated them with caution. We got caught in one once before and it was pretty scary for me. The local people warned us some skiffs had capsized as they tried to make it through Akun Straight, fighting those riptides. While Hans may have been better at navigating, he was also more daring; Charlie was always in charge of running the boat through the Straight when they were together.

Uncle Paul's elder brother, Bill McGlashan, a tall gray-haired man in his seventies who went by Uncle Bill, had a small fishing cabin on Akun, which he no longer used. One afternoon we went to his home where he and his very friendly wife, Aunt Polly to everyone, lived with Anesia's family. As we sat at the kitchen table, he wrote out a bill of sale on paper from a small spiral note pad that would fit in a man's pocket, the same kind of paper as Uncle Paul's Will. Village life was uncomplicated. Uncle Bill wanted seventy-five dollars, not much money, but worth more in 1965 than in the twenty-first century. Now the guys would have a little better place to stay when the weather was bad or when they had to stay over a few days because of the work they had to do.

They stocked the little cabin with canned and dry goods, cooking utensils and their sleeping bags. While the tiny cabin wasn't very comfortable, the shearing shed was even less. Sometimes villagers used it when they got stranded due to weather, and they also helped replenish the supplies.

When they finished the shearing on Akun the guys spent more time on Akutan at the head of the bay finishing the barn. There wasn't a lot of time left and it had to be done without power tools—the old fashioned way—but they still had some long daylight hours, when it wasn't overcast or foggy. The barn was close to the beach to cut down on the hauling distance for supplies. With no motorized vehicles, everything had to be done manually.

The bay was shallow for a long way out, so the tide had to be high to run the dory up the beach as far as possible to shorten the distance to the barn. Because the dory sat high and dry during low tide, they tried to plan trips around the tides, though sometimes they couldn't wait and had to push and pull the heavy twenty-two footer down to the water, not an easy task even for two strong men.

The completed barn looked more like a wood frame cabin with its gable roof, though it had no windows. The inside was mostly unfinished with no ceiling, just bare rafters, and no insulation between the two by fours. Inside and out, the structure had a gray weathered look as we had brought a huge pile of salvaged material with us on the *MV Robert Eugene*. The front door, an old wooden relic, came from an abandoned building. They attached plywood platforms on two by fours for bunks along the sidewalls on either side of the door for when the bay was too rough and unsafe to make the two-mile trip back to town.

We brought a small second-hand oil cook stove with us. The oven door required a board propped between it and the floor to hold it shut; the rest of it was in good condition. It was placed in the barn as a source of heat on the chilly nights they spent there, and it also kept a tea kettle hot for their cowboy coffee (boiling water with fresh coffee grounds thrown in).

Once the barn was closed in, we removed the tarps from the piles of hay, bags of feed and other supplies that we'd piled on the ground and moved everything into the new structure. Hay filled the back half of the barn from the dirt floor to the uninsulated rafters. The rest of the supplies and equipment took up a lot of the remaining space.

Unlike the horses, the cows remained at the head of the bay most of that summer, but when the increased activity began in their front yard, some of them moved further and further away, though still within sight. Small amounts of hay were scattered near the site to discourage them from becoming too adventurous. One afternoon just after it turned dark, Charlie and Hans returned home as I was just ending classes. When I entered our apartment, Hans was stretched out on the couch and Charlie was settled in the recliner. Neither of them spoke, just gave me glum looks. I didn't like that.

"Okay, what's going on? Did we lose another cow?"

Charlie said, "Not exactly. It was just getting light when we got there to work on the barn and we noticed there didn't appear to be as many cows. Then when we looked around some more we noticed that several cows were part way up the steep hill that leads to Hot Springs Bay on the other side. As we looked further up we saw one almost to the top of that five hundred foot ridge."

"Yah, and two following it, though much further down," Hans added.

About a mile and a half north of the barn, and beyond that steep east-west ridge, is Hot Springs Bay, one of the by-products of an active volcano on the island, generically named Akutan Volcano. It was behind our property and about six miles west of the village. The hills around Hot Springs Bay formed a horseshoe-shaped valley about two miles wide containing several hot springs that provided warmth and good grazing. It had just been a matter of time before some curious cow moved up the sloping swampy terrain to see what was on the other side of that high ridge, with some of the others following close behind.

Charlie continued, "We took off running through the spongy moss to get them to turn around. When we reached the lowest one we got it headed back down, but the one nearest the top moved faster and was soon out of sight over the ridge. The other one also picked up speed and seemed to be pretty surefooted for that climb. That animal was just too far ahead for us to reach it but we followed it anyway at a slower pace and saw it reach the top. When we made it to the ridge, both cows were moving downward far ahead of us, the first one almost to the bottom. We spotted another cow already down there and grazing. Then we headed back to our herd and counted them and were only missing three."

"Yah, first thing ve did vas put out more hay near the barn. Ve figured if the other three didn't come back right away, ve'd have to spend a day trying to coax them back." Hans looked tired and unhappy.

They made more trips that fall and tried to bring them back as it would be much easier to help the cows with calving if they were closer to the barn, but it was to no avail. When winter set in the herd was split almost in half; some opted for the comfortable warm springs, though the hay the guys put out near the barn lured others. When snow covered the ridge, Charlie and Hans took the skiff around the island to Hot Springs Bay to check on the rest of herd, but the cows appeared okay without any extra feeding.

The guys completed the main building projects just ahead of the early snows, but our cabin wasn't one of them. It wasn't even begun. When I argued the need for at least putting in the piling foundation, so they could work on the framing in the winter, they claimed they lost a lot of time trying to unite the herd, and now the weather was snowy and there was little daylight.

"So what did you accomplish? You didn't get those cows out of Hot Springs Bay and you haven't started our cabin." My voice continued to rise. "This is hard work for me working long hours. You won't see me sitting around with any free time. Are you going to crowd us back into Uncle Paul's next summer?"

There's a fine line between annoyance and anger, so I'm not sure if my lack of patience was giving way to an increasing annoyance or if it was anger over the way the ranch project was gaining a foothold inside me. Perhaps because I had a 'real job' with a guaranteed salary, I was expressing myself far more than I had at the inception of the ranch idea. I'd left the planning to the two green cowboys and naively had looked on the whole idea as 'a great adventure.' In my ignorance, I'd relied solely on the two of them to work out all the details. In retrospect, I should have asked more questions, helped more with the logistics, been more involved, not just with getting the animals here, but with the 'what next' phase.

One weekend morning in late October Charlie said, "We won't be going to the head of the bay anymore as we've done all we can till spring."

I was startled. "What! When did you decide that?"

Charlie looked at Hans and then said, "Well, Hans has a chance to go fishing and we can use the extra money."

"Yah, one of the skippers that come in here said he'd take me on as a deck hand this next veek. They're fishing king crab out of Dutch Harbor so I vouldn't be that far avay. It's just for a few months."

"Well, what about the cabin? Can't you get something started on it?"

Charlie said, "We got this schoolhouse apartment to live in till the end of May. We can start our cabin in the spring."

"You should start something now. There'll be lots of spring projects that'll take priority over our cabin." When I got no response from either of them, I added, "Are you thinking you could just put us back in Uncle Paul's? I didn't mind three months, but it wasn't in the original plan to remain in the village. We were going to have our own place, and live on our own property."

Neither of them said anything. I took that as my answer. It added to my own disillusion about the ranch. I felt they'd already discussed it between themselves and were stalling on committing to the cabin. I left them sitting in the living room and went in the bedroom.

A week later, Hans left on a fishing boat, his first experience as a deck hand. Charlie spent a little time looking after the large school generator, along with one of the local men who also took care of it when Charlie was gone. I worked long hours in the classroom, and with no 'free period' during the day, spent my evenings and weekends grading papers and making the puzzle-like lesson plans to cover all eight grades and their multiple subjects.

I was angry that Charlie didn't discuss any plan about a place for us when school ended, and if I entered the apartment during the day for something, Charlie was often sitting on the couch reading, finishing one book then starting another. If he wasn't there, he was off in the village visiting. But he made no trip to the head of the bay.

His behavior infuriated me and the tension continued to build between us. Instead of bringing us closer together, the ranch seemed to be driving us apart.

"Why can't you get something started on our cabin? I'm working long hours. I'm providing us a place to live and a paycheck. What are you doing? I don't think it's fair." I must have sounded like the proverbial nagging wife. I certainly had the dialogue down pat.

He had no argument, gave no excuse, just got up and left to go visit one of the guys. I didn't like that change in him. His show of indifference only added to my annoyance.

Hans returned to Akutan for short periods during the next few months, since he wasn't fishing that far away. On one of those visits, I told him of my problems with Charlie, that he'd always been a hard worker before coming here. I didn't know how much more of the situation I could take. I was very frustrated. Hans agreed that something was wrong, but said he would talk to Charlie and see what was going on.

I appreciated his understanding of the problem. Charlie was his partner and they were in the ranch together. Our family 'adopted' Hans, then twenty-nine, as a brother, uncle, and best friend, not just as a ranch partner, so I knew he would like to see our family unit remain intact. From the stories he told us, he hadn't experienced a very settled life, nor had he felt he was a part of a real family till we took him in. He told of a difficult time growing up. I assured him that he was still a part of the children's lives and I considered him my best friend even without the ranch.

He was born in Konigsberg, East Prussia in 1935, though Konigsberg and East Prussia ceased to exist after World War II. Prior to the war, Konigsberg was a great cultural center, with a population of about three hundred fifty thousand and many architecturally beautiful buildings centuries old. His father was a baker, who was conscripted into the German army and killed on the Russian front when Hans was six and his sister was four. His mother never remarried and struggled to raise the two young children doing odd jobs, since she had limited education.

Because East Prussia was a German province, the Royal Air Force, a branch of the British armed forces, incinerated the city in 1944. The survivors were then overrun by the Soviet Red Army in 1945 who claimed the province as its own and changed Konigsberg, East Prussia to Kaliningrad, Russia.

In 1944, at age nine, Hans, his seven year old sister and his mother, having survived the destruction of the city, boarded a huge transport ship on the Baltic Sea with about five thousand other refugees escaping just ahead of the Russian army. The boat was headed for the American sector, and eventually Bremen. Hans claimed one of his worst experiences growing up was on that huge overcrowded refugee boat, when he got separated from his mother and sister for three days and had only what food strangers could spare the frightened little boy who had just fled his destroyed home only to find himself wandering through a mass of thousands of people for three days, looking for his mother.

Eventually they went to live on a pig farm near Bremen. When he was old enough, his mother put him in a painter's apprentice school, an intensive four year program. He had hoped to go to high school but his mother insisted he was better off learning a trade so he could support the three of them. He wasn't happy about it but as it turned out his training provided him with enough jobs to leave Germany and immigrate to America.

Though he traveled many places in the world from his Alaska home base, he never returned to Germany, and didn't even like being considered a German. He had a pronounced accent, though, and always said 've' for 'we', among other improperly pronounced words. But when people asked him what nationality he was, he always proudly replied, "American."

His traumatic childhood experiences probably had a lot to do with being so willing to become a part of our family. With all the pitfalls we encountered in less than a year on Akutan, he never expressed any regrets.

7

Aleut Christmas

As the holiday season approached, several of the women stopped by our apartment one evening and told me how the villagers observed Christmas in their village, specifically Christmas Eve. Traditionally, they used the schoolhouse for a community celebration. There would be no cutting of a Christmas tree, mainly because trees were not native to the island. If one ever was planted and survived, it was unthinkable that anyone would kill it for a festival. They told me that there was a large artificial tree in the school storage shed that some of the people would come by and set up in the classroom. Knowing this, I could make plans to clear a spot as they said the tree was rather large. As the women continued to inform me about the event they told me that shortly before Christmas Eve, all the families brought their presents to the school and placed them under the tree, rather than handing them out in their own homes. In 1965, with no more than fifteen houses, and many people related by blood or marriage, spending Christmas Eve together sounded like a huge family celebration, very festive! Besides tree space, my mind began expanding the allotted area. But it was a big room and we could work it out.

The children spent lots of free time decorating the classroom once the tree was up. With their understandable restlessness I tried to keep them busy. It didn't help that various adults showed up with bags of gifts that they placed under the tree. Before class and during recess the students couldn't stay away from the tree. When they found their names on some of the tags, I heard remarks like, "Oh boy! Another one for me."

I knew it was a waste of time no matter how emphatically I said it, when I told them, "Do not go through the presents." If they were being tested to see if they could resist temptation, they failed.

I planned my gifts to my students well in advance. Those were the days of the Sears Christmas Catalog, which many of us in the bush eagerly awaited every fall. I sent my order in early to allow for the slow shipping and frequent plane delays. The catalog offered sweat shirts plus a kit for iron- on letters, so I ordered twenty-five navy blue pullovers in sizes small, medium, and large, and the letter kit to iron on their first names in big white letters. Though it strapped my budget somewhat, I wanted to use that opportunity to let them know how special they were to me. Without a clothing store there, they always seemed so appreciative when they got new clothes. Also, I wanted their gifts to be something personal. They showed their thanks by wearing them to school frequently: however, with their names printed on them, I hadn't counted on the pullovers being handed down when they outgrew them.

Besides the traditional American Christmas, the community celebrated the Russian Orthodox Christmas. Their small white church was at the opposite end of the village from the school. The interior was well maintained by some of the village men. A beautiful spotless red carpet covered the floor. With no vacuum cleaner, they cleaned it by hand, sometimes on their hands and knees. They showed a lot of pride and respect for their church. Upon entering, one would see various colorful gold-tinted icons of Jesus and saintly 'fathers of the Church', and believers who were considered to have led devout lives. Infrequently, a priest would visit and provide a service. More often, one of the local men, referred to as a reader, conducted the readings and some very beautiful singing, chants actually, that I enjoyed hearing when I was invited on special occasions. Since I was not a member they didn't expect my presence except at such times, but I always felt privileged when invited.

Besides religious services over the holidays, there were other events. One was called starring. A large star, three or four feet high, was colorfully decorated and carried to all the houses. That first year the reader, an older man, was in charge, though younger people carried it. When they arrived at the houses, they went in and the one in charge led them in religious songs. Each house had food set out, often cakes, pies, cookies or candies. But sometimes it was bread, stew or fish. Anyone could go with them as they carried the star from house to house. I was invited to join after they left the schoolhouse, though I didn't know their songs. It was a treat to witness this unique custom.

The holiday activity that I enjoyed the most was 'masking.' I had never heard of it until one of my older students, Darryl, explained it to me and invited me to join them. The custom was common in Aleut villages, and involved wearing a mask and dancing. It took place between Christmas and New Year's. I don't know its religious significance but supposedly they went to church later. Mostly what I gathered was that it had some similarities to Halloween, which also started out as a religious activity, though involving a different religious event. It seemed simple enough to me and sounded like it might be fun. I was in for a surprise. I don't know how it was conducted in other villages, but I found out firsthand how it was practiced in Akutan, in 1965. They told me the first thing I had to do was take a large old pillow case and cut out two tiny eye holes, just enough to see where I was going. I would be wearing it over my head, hence the name, 'masking.' Some maskers decorated their pillow cases with colored markers, drawing in eyebrows, nose, moustache, etc. The object was to hide one's identity from the people whose houses we would visit. Naturally, pillow cases were not sufficient. Masking required full body disguise. The students agreed not to tell anyone that I was going to participate. They came to the schoolhouse to get me that evening.

Those of us that participated as maskers, about ten men and women, plus a few of the older students, and one school teacher, myself, met in a small almost empty building, called the community hall, which looked sort of like a warehouse. A gray pasteboard barrel about three feet high was filled with all kinds of old clothes that looked like leftovers from a rummage sale. The clothes were kept there for maskers and each year some of the clothing that was too worn was thrown out, and replaced by more old clothes. Yes, the village was into recycling back in '65, long before it became fashionable. We dumped out the clothes, picked oversized garments, and began to get dressed, or I should say padded. We had to wear clothing with long sleeves and wide pant legs, since we tied twine around the ends of them to hold in all the extra clothing we wadded up and stuffed in them to completely disguise our bodies. More was jammed down the front and back and a cloth belt helped hold everything in place. Then we put on oversized boots stuffed with paper and rags and pulled on our masks. The last items to go on were padded work gloves that looked like something Mickey Mouse would wear.

By now, we could hardly move, but we managed to waddle out the door and head for the first house in total silence. One masker carried a portable 45 rpm record player. Somewhere else we might have looked like a strange group, since it was long past Halloween. We were certainly not a sight anyone would open their door to, especially on a dark December night, except in Akutan where the villagers were prepared for masking.

Masking was a guessing game. We would enter each house in total silence, encased in our disguises and the people would try to guess who we were, and if they succeeded in identifying someone, that person had to unmask. We knocked at the first house, and then entered silently when the door opened. The record player was turned on and the 45 rpm record started playing polka music. We sort of danced with each other, though it wasn't really dancing. We just held onto each other's shoulders and rocked back and forth from one oversized stuffed boot to the other. While we did this those watching tried to make us laugh so they could guess whose voice it was. Sometimes it was hard for me not to laugh, just seeing the others rocking about like fat robots. But most of us persevered. Only a few got unmasked for laughing.

Each house placed food on a table for the maskers, sometimes cookies and tea, maybe slices of cake, and occasionally some stew. The residents

Our first winter at Akutan, 1966. The village is seen from across the bay.

weren't trying to show hospitality, they were trying to get a glimpse of us as we struggled to eat or drink. We lowered each item to the bottom of our masks, slipped it under and then raised it to our lips. We did pretty well even with our sausage fingers, though they watched us closely. As we proceeded from house to house, our costumes were getting pretty well stained from our sloppy eating. We developed an entourage as some people from previous houses followed us and went in with us. In such a little community it was a big event.

With only a few houses remaining, about half the group was unmasked, though they stayed with us. The rest of us had hopes of making it to the end with our pillow cases still on our heads. As absurd as that sounds, that would be our reward. We were almost home free when we went into a house that had set a trap for us. After we finished bouncing back and forth to about three minutes of canned noise, we were told to sit at a table that had been set with bowls and spoons. Then they served us sea lion stew, knowing

Spring of '66, there is little snow remaining. Looking toward the head of the bay from the village, the sewage system is evident in the foreground.

it would be difficult to slip it under our masks. I'd never eaten sea lion meat though it had been offered me. The fishy smell did not seem appetizing when I went into a house where it was cooking. I could smell it now as I was served a steaming bowl of it. The cooked meat had a dark gray look, but I knew I had to at least try it. I carried a spoonful to the bottom of the pillow case in order to get it underneath, and then managed to get it up to my mouth without spilling most of it. While it was very messy, the others were having the same problem, and had wet stains all over their masks. Our hosts made fun of us for the ridiculous way we ate, and talked among them about who they thought we were.

Looking at me, someone said, "I thought that was Mrs. Brown, but she wouldn't eat the sea lion meat."

That was all the encouragement I needed. I cleaned my bowl. By the time we reached the last house, though, we were all unmasked. We were actually grateful as we were hot with all that padding plus a cloth bag over our heads, not to mention the stuffed gloves. But simple pleasures have their own rewards.

In 1965, Christmas in Akutan was a unique experience and had helped keep me from dwelling so much on our ranch situation and family problems. But that was a temporary reprieve, and as the season came to an end and classes resumed my concerns returned.

Chapter

8

Springtime in Akutan

After the Christmas vacation, classes returned to the pre-holiday routine with one exception. A special class was added. The state legislature mandated that the villages should have a class in their native language as part of preserving their culture.

The villagers chose a new chief from time to time, sort of like an honorary mayor. That year it was Bill Tcheripanoff, a slender man in his sixties who always wore a bill cap, and often presented a rather serious demeanor. He accepted the job of teaching the Aleut language to the class. He came twice a week for about half an hour each time. As I observed the class occasionally I could tell the native heritage meant a great deal to him as he told of the 'old ways' when he was young. I felt he was probably the right person for the job.

Aleut was already spoken in all of the homes; some of the older people didn't speak or read English very well. Out of a courtesy to their elders, and a need to be understood, the children often spoke Aleut around them, though there were still lots of words they didn't know. Someday these same children would have to pass on the language if it was to survive. Since many of my students had learned English as a second language, perhaps that accounted for the lack of reading material in some of the homes. The students certainly took advantage of all the books on our library shelf. Like my daughter, a prolific reader, many of them were engrossed in reading whenever they had free time.

When WWII spread to the Aleutians, the older people now living in the Akutan village were evacuated from their island homes and placed in internment camps several thousand miles away. They were told it was for their safety, but the living conditions they were subjected to were deplorable and inexcusable. When they returned to their homes after the end of the war there was little to go back to in the way of housing as so much was vandalized, and personal possessions that they had not been allowed to take with them were 'missing.' Schooling opportunities were limited while they had been in the camps. During the time I lived there, none of those residents living in the village had completed high school, though I was told that some of the children who completed eighth grade went off to high school elsewhere and just didn't return to the island. I would think there were various reasons, but perhaps it was mainly the limited opportunities and the isolation. Despite the elders' lack of formal schooling, they encouraged the young people in all of their educational endeavors, which in part accounted for Bill's willingness to help.

Bill, well into his sixties, did more than just teach them words, he lectured on the 'old' ways, how life used to be before the advent of so many white people with their own culture. Bill let me know he wasn't very fond of the outsiders and it didn't seem to matter to him that I was considered white (my mother was Hispanic), he had to vent his frustration over the white man's influence. I don't know if he had a dislike for them; I think it was more of a nostalgia / sadness that is sometimes all that is left of the past. I can sympathize as I see that my Akutan of old has not been spared and now lives pretty much in my memory.

In spite of his misgivings, he was generally pretty friendly to me and we got along well. Maybe that was why he felt he could express his feelings more openly. Of course, he remembered my assistance on the day of my arrival, the day his granddaughter died and my all- night vigil with his grandson. But we never spoke of it.

While Bill took over the class, I was able to grade papers and do lesson plans, so I appreciated the break in my day. He liked working with the children and wanted them to know about their heritage. However, as the months went by, Bill stopped showing up on a regular basis as he got busier and busier with the approach of fishing season and other spring activities. No one else wanted to replace him, as they were also involved in similar projects. But for a little while some of Bill's knowledge was passed on. Even Becky and Malcolm benefited from his work with the class and were able to understand some of the words their classmates used among themselves, especially when they didn't want me to know what they were saying.

Boats continued to fish for king crab that winter in all kinds of weather, as the crab meat was considered a delicacy and commanded a high premium. A few years before, the majority of the king crab left Kodiak waters and moved to the Dutch Harbor area, so when Hans returned from fishing in late January, Charlie took a deck hand job on an old Portuguese crab fishing boat out of Dutch, the *F/V Santa Maria*. A small chapel on the boat was an interesting remnant of the strong religious beliefs of the early Portuguese sailors. Now it provided a place of solitude for the fishermen as they risked their lives in one of the most turbulent fishing grounds in Alaska.

One afternoon that winter while Charlie was still gone and Hans was over at Akun doing some work, some men wearing dripping raingear barged into my classroom. Without any formality, one man announced, "We have a badly injured deckhand. Akutan was the nearest village and we heard the schoolteacher was also a nurse. Is that you?" The man spoke rapidly and with a note of desperation.

I had hurried to the back of the classroom when he entered. "Yes, that's me. I'm Mrs. Brown."

"We want to bring the man into your apartment and maybe you could take a look at him. He's in bad shape."

"Of course. Get him in there on the couch. Robert and Eva, take over. Dismiss them when it's time. I'll be right next door if you need me." With that, I followed the fisherman into my living room.

Several men carried an unconscious man through the door and placed him on the couch, which was against the window that faced the Bay. While they took off some of his heavy wet clothing and fishing boots, I checked the injured man's vital signs. Clear fluid drained from one ear. He appeared quite young, around nineteen or twenty, and lighter complexioned than the weather-seasoned fishermen whose skin had been toughened by much exposure to wind and salt water spray. When they removed his watch-cap I noticed he had short light curly hair, which added to his youthful appearance.

The skipper said, "I notified the Naval Base at Kodiak and they're sending a rescue plane, the Albatross. It should be on its way as it's been awhile since I called. There's still some daylight." He didn't sound totally convinced about the last as that was cutting it close. There was little I could do except keep the man warm and check his vitals from time to time.

"What happened?" I asked, as I covered the young man with a blanket.

The skipper said, "He was hit by a crab pot as it swayed overhead on a boom, while the boat was jogging in some pretty big waves."

A king crab pot is a seven foot by seven foot by three foot box frame, which I would guess could hold eight or nine tall men with room left over, huge. Made of steel, they weigh about seven hundred fifty pounds. The frame is covered with special mesh and is designed to trap the crab when they enter the pot to get the bait. As the pots are being hauled from or dropped into the water they sometimes swing wildly, especially in rough seas, and fishermen have to constantly be on the alert to avoid them. King crab fishing is a dangerous occupation, one of the most dangerous in the country. Hardly a year goes by without a boat going down or a man being lost at sea. The high mortality rate is a major factor in the price of king crab. The incentive had to be big enough for men to risk their lives.

"After the deckhand was hit, those two," he motioned to the other two fishermen who sat on kitchen chairs in the living room, looking solemn, "raced toward him and grabbed him. He was unconscious and sliding toward the railing. Then they laid him on the deck and held him there as the boat kept rising and falling in the rough water. Those guys moved fast and saved the kid from being washed overboard. We weren't far from Akutan, so we headed here. I told the Kodiak base we'd be here. We went next door to the house with the marine radio, and that's when Agnes Feller told us that you were also a nurse. So we came right over here."

When school ended for the day, Becky and Malcolm came into our apartment. They were very quiet when they saw the unconscious man. Becky at age nine took on the cooking and baking duties for the family and was very good at it. She relied heavily on my old *Better Homes and Gardens* cookbook. I told her what to prepare for our dinner and she went right to work on the meal while Malcolm went straight to their bedroom and got out his little plastic soldiers that he liked to play with when he was alone. They both sensed that something serious had happened.

Eventually, the Albatross streamed across the water just as it started to get dark. The tension in the room eased as the men started conversing more and also stopped whispering. They bundled up the deckhand in his now almost dry clothing and wrapped him in a blanket, then thanked me for my hospitality, though I hadn't done much except 'be there.' Then they headed down to their skiff and went out to the sea plane where there would be a doctor plus medical supplies on board. I never learned if the injured man survived, but I was glad for the Navy's availability and quick response in a medical emergency. In later years the Kodiak base would become a Coast Guard base and they would take over those duties.

Living inside the school apartment, I spent an increasing amount of time in the classroom working on assignments in order to avoid the stressful tension I felt when Charlie and I were in the same room. I'd never witnessed Charlie's indifference to work that needed to be done, just sitting around. He had always been a hard worker, putting in long hours in bad weather on various jobs. I hadn't seen this side of him in the ten years we had been married, so I couldn't recognize the symptoms of what was going on—his growing depression—and he seemed oblivious to symptoms of my heart breaking as my own discouragement set in. I now saw the futility of our relationship along with the problems with the ranch.

On a lighter side, I did come up with a form of entertainment for my family and the villagers. Amenities that were lacking at the time were movies and television, which further emphasized our remoteness from the modern world. I had an old sixteen millimeter projector that I brought with me from Dutch Harbor, not so much because I had planned to show movies as the fact that we had brought everything we owned to Akutan.

At that time, we sincerely believed it would be our final home—no more moves. Once I remembered the projector, stored down at Uncle Paul's cabin, I got it out and looked in an Anchorage phone book we had kept with us. I found a company that rented 16mm movies to people in the bush and to processors and work camps. I contacted them and received a list of their movies and selected one to arrive on each plane, so twice a month I showed them to the local people—one more reason to look forward to 'plane day.' We watched them in the classroom and most of the villagers came, some bringing popcorn and soda pop. I provided the movies free as I would have ordered them for my family, anyway, and was happy to share with everyone.

Captains Courageous, with Spencer Tracy, a black and white 1939 tearjerker, was one of my favorites, though it made most of us cry. The father of some of my students, Nick Borenin, came up to me as he wiped away tears and said, "That was too sad." I was wiping my eyes, too. But I liked it so much I showed it again the following week since we had to wait another week for a plane, and most of the people showed up. We all cried a second time. I can still hear little Freddie Barthalomew shouting, "Manuel! Manuel!" when Tracy is fatally injured and my eyes get watery. Sometimes we like to torture ourselves.

Charlie returned to Akutan after a little over a month of fishing. The *FV Santa Maria* had to hole up in protected coves and bays a lot of the time due to the winter storms, so he didn't make much money, but it was better than having him sit around in the apartment reading books and visiting with fishermen and bringing in no money at all. Also, that was a month of no arguing which had been a drain on me, as the long school hours took their own toll. Hans took off again on a crab boat when Charlie got back and said he would be gone till early spring when the chores on Akun would start.

The weather warmed, heavy spring rains pelted the snow and everything seemed to progress in a routine manner. Springtime is considered the time for the renewal of the species; ewes give birth to lambs and cows give birth to calves. I, too, was renewing my species, though mine wouldn't take place till August, as I was expecting my third child. I guess I fell a little behind the animal cycle. But it gave me time to finish my teaching contract and make arrangements for housing in Anchorage, about eight hundred miles away, where I planned to go for our new arrival.

I expected to remain in Anchorage as I was unhappy, discouraged and exhausted. I felt I could no longer deal with Charlie's behavior. I had friends in Anchorage and it was a fair sized city so I knew I could find some kind of work. I felt I could not count on any money from the ranch, or Charlie for that matter. He didn't seem interested in seeking any work before shearing and made no move to go to the head of the bay and start on the cabin even though he knew I was expecting another child.

The situation was very tense when we were together, and we spoke very little. But one thing we made a point of, we did not argue in front of the children. I hadn't even told them I didn't plan to return. They knew I had to leave to have the baby; they didn't know we wouldn't be coming back. They were very happy with their life on Akutan. Less than a year into the ranch and very little had gone as expected. I had experienced a wonderful year living on the island and had made some very good friends. I didn't really want to leave all that but there was no work for me there and I would have three children depending on me. I didn't count on any help from their father. I had never seen him behave like this. So many times I wanted to cry, but I couldn't let my children know; I wanted to keep that knowledge from them as long as possible. I planned to file for a divorce after we got to Anchorage. Charlie didn't try to talk me out of it; he reacted as if he didn't care. He didn't even want to discuss it. His indifference was strange behavior for him.

When I informed Hans of all that was going on, he agreed with what I was seeing as he had also observed it and didn't understand what had happened to his partner.

"Do you tink I'm blind? I don't know vat's going on? I'll try to talk to him but I don't know if it'll do any good. I know you have to leave, but I hope Charlie vill snap out of it. I vant to make da ranch vork."

Chapter

9

Swamp Delivery

One $rainy$ afternoon in April, while school was still in progress, two young men from the village darted into my classroom, water dripping from their dark rubber raingear. Only an extraordinary event would compel any of the local people to rush in during class, so it was obvious that something was wrong. I hurried to the back of the room where they stood in the doorway, Tommy McGlashan and Ignaty Philamonoff, both a few years younger than me.

Breathing hard, Tommy, usually sociable and outgoing, exclaimed excitedly, "Mrs. Brown! We've just come from the head of the bay! One of your cows is having a calf!"

While that is not an everyday occurrence, I wondered why the men seemed so upset. Ignaty, the older brother of my eighth grade student, Eva, wiped the rain from his face and blurted, "But just the calf's legs are sticking out and that cow is bellowing like crazy! We tried to get near her but she kept moving away." Ignaty was usually a bit shy around me, though not unfriendly, so those were probably the most words he had spoken to me. He would soon break that record and a stronger relationship would be cemented.

Tommy sounded a little calmer now as he attempted to recruit my help. "We know Charlie and Hans are in Unalaska till tomorrow, but we don't know what to do. We never delivered a calf but I think that cow needs help! We came to see if you could do something."

I led them to the back of the room and Tommy continued, "We'd been duck hunting in a swampy area at the head of the bay when suddenly we heard a loud noise that repeated itself over and over. As we followed the sound, from a distance we saw a cow standing up to her belly in about a foot of muddy water. She looked really miserable."

It sounded to me like a breach presentation, coming out legs first like that. I knew it was a serious complication, but my nursing experience in obstetrics involved only human deliveries. I'd never delivered a calf, and though I had observed a few normal bovine deliveries, my knowledge of breach deliveries was limited to our veterinary handbook.

At five foot one, one hundred ten pounds, and five months pregnant, I really wanted to decline. But I saw in their anxious faces the same feelings of helplessness that I felt in that unfamiliar situation. It was my responsibility, not theirs, though I didn't know how much help I could be. I sensed they were willing to assist me, but they were uncomfortable going it alone and probably thought I would be more knowledgeable, a mistaken assumption. Though Charlie was raised on a Hereford cattle ranch in New Mexico, I was raised in the heart of Kansas City where cows were not a common occurrence except in the foul-smelling stockyards. I felt nervous about the situation, but I knew what I had to do.

I put my two dependable eighth graders, Robert and Eva, in charge, as only about fifteen minutes remained before dismissal. I grabbed my heavy parka, with its fur-trimmed hood, pulled on calf length rubber boots, and got our vet book out of the apartment. I planned to take a crash course in animal delivery complications while riding in the boat. I dashed down to the long wooden dory through a cold light rain and climbed in; I was still somewhat agile at five months. Ignaty ran the engine full throttle as I sat shivering in that open boat pelted by salt spray that flew off the bow. In spite of the fast bumpy ride I managed to read a few paragraphs on animal obstetrics, just enough to know the information would be useless.

As we drew closer to the beach, I could make out the miserable animal in the distance. Sure enough, she was standing right in the swamp, about a hundred yards from our barn, which was on solid ground. If we could get her over to it things would be easier and more convenient for all concerned.

When we reached shore the boat's momentum shot the dory far up the beach. We climbed over the side and trudged through the mist toward the bizarre scene that presented itself. Tommy and Ignaty were about Charlie's height—five foot eight—and in better physical shape than me, so it didn't take them long to get pretty far ahead. As I caught up to where they had stopped, I could make out the two long spindly legs protruding from the cow and was unnerved by the pitiful bellowing, magnified by the stillness of the swamp.

The three of us waded toward her with muddy water half way up our boots, but the cow took off in the opposite direction from the barn. In spite of her critical situation, neither the two long-legged young men nor I in my cumbersome condition could even get close to her. The deep swamp made it difficult to move very fast—unless you were a cow!

Tommy, always the assertive one, said, "I'll go look in the barn for some rope and maybe we can make some sort of lasso." He soon rejoined us with a rope, which he knotted to form a loop. After many attempts and much tromping through muddy water, the guys finally succeeded in getting the rope around her—but then she refused to budge. By then she had led us even deeper into the swamp, where animal and humans stood in about a foot and a half of cold water, with thick soft mud underneath. Since she outweighed the three of us combined, we were forced to provide assistance in that most inconvenient location.

Ignaty in his quiet way said little, but looked at me with a reassuring smile on his thin lips, his black eyes glinting like polished onyx in his narrow face. I felt confident he meant to help me through this uncharted experience, and I was grateful.

Slipping and sliding, we struggled to keep our footing in the dark water as two of us held tightly to the rope while the third attempted to dislodge the fetus. But it would not move, and the huge bovine continued her loud agonized cries. Periodically, we rotated positions, holding the rope or pulling on the calf.

I found it hard to get traction on the slippery mud, so my feet often slid out from under me, causing me to land flat on my back as the cold dirty water flooded the inside of my boots, ran down my collar, and up my sleeves. My tangled shoulder length auburn hair was a mass of mud, and water streaked down my face, but I didn't dare let go of the rope, so I used my waterlogged sleeve to wipe myself. The skin on my hands became raw from pulling so hard on the rough fiber rope, as I hadn't taken time to grab gloves when I picked up the veterinary book. Maybe I thought I would just need the book and act as a consultant to those guys. I should have got gloves instead.

As darkness set in we became mere shadows to each other, gyrating gray silhouettes in a forbidding landscape. After a while, perhaps to relieve the built-up tension and to bury thoughts of our tired muscles, we laughed at the absurdity of the scene, though we knew it was too serious to be funny.

Several hours after we left the schoolhouse, Tommy, almost on his back in the swamp, was able to dislodge the fetus. Then he stood holding the bloody-looking bundle of animal bones, not with an expression of triumph, but with look of sadness as he said, "Thank God!" Judging by the calf's macerated appearance it had been dead for some time. The outcome was anticipated, though disappointing. However, I was thankful the miserable cow no longer had to endure the pain. Her gut-wrenching sounds had ceased and the swamp quickly returned to its eerie stillness.

Ignaty and I continued to hold the rope till Tommy carried the dead calf to the dory. Tommy told us the cow's maternal instinct would cause her to stay with the dead animal if we just left it. Soon Tommy hollered back to us, "You can let her go now."

I was thankful to quit pulling on it since I now had more time to focus on how much my arms ached. Ignaty did the rope removal as I relaxed my hold, then he slipped it from the cow's head. She immediately headed farther away from us, and in the misty darkness soon disappeared from our vision.

Ignaty coiled the wet rope, then shoved a wet dripping lock of hair from his forehead. "Thanks, Ignaty. I really appreciated your help and Tommy's. I won't forget this." I felt deeply indebted to the two of them.

As he left with the rope to head for the barn he said, "I'm sorry about the calf."

I plodded slowly through the swamp toward the beach where Tommy waited. I was anxious to leave that lonely place.

After Ignaty and I climbed into the boat with rivulets of swamp mud dripping from our hair and clothes, Tommy shoved the boat off the beach and jumped aboard; then Ignaty yanked the cord to start the outboard motor. The overwhelming events of the past few hours seemed to cast a pall over us. We rode in silence as the boat moved at a much slower speed through the dark waters. The misty rain felt refreshing after wallowing in swamp water. It was a sad ending to our efforts, but I took comfort in the knowledge that the two men, unasked, reached out to help me deal with what would have been an impossible situation without help.

10

Spring Disaster

Charlie and Hans headed for Akun in the spring to get ready for shearing. Because we had no communication between the two islands in those days, they told me they would be over there awhile, at least a few weeks as they had lots of work to do now that the snow was gone. The first lamb crop was due plus the shearing shed had to be set up for all the shearing.

A few days later, when Charlie showed up in the classroom doorway wearing his yellow waterproof bib overalls, his grim expression told me something was seriously wrong. My first thought was that something bad had happened to Hans.

"Joan, I have to talk to you," he said, and went into the apartment.

I hurried to the back of the classroom, and then followed him into our living room. "What's wrong? Has something happened to Hans?"

Talking fast in a voice mixed with sadness and disbelief, Charlie told me the bad news.

"Hans is okay but the sheep aren't. When we arrived at Akun, we saw many sheep carcasses scattered around the island. Some were alive but lying on their side, so heavy with wool they were unable to right themselves.

It was a terrible sight. We didn't know what to make of it. Hans and I stood up as many as we could, but some were so weak they just fell over again. But others began to move slowly and seemed to get their strength back as they began grazing. We don't know what's wrong with them. We've never heard of anything like this."

"This is crazy," I said in disbelief. "This doesn't make any sense at all. It's been weeks since you were over there. Why didn't you check again before now? This didn't happen overnight." I felt the anger surge in me. I stared at him. I was stunned. I should have been more sympathetic, but I had too much pent up anger about Charlie's and my situation.

"Maybe they got some kind of disease that spread through the flock. I don't know. I'm going to call Milt at the Chernofski ranch and see if he can shed some light on this mess. We couldn't find anything in the vet book. After I get hold of him, I'll stop back and let you know what he has to say; then I got to get back to Akun while there's still some daylight to get through the pass."

"Everything's gone wrong with this ranch!" I started to cry. They were angry tears.

"You better go take care of your class." Charlie turned toward the door.

He headed over to Aggie Feller's next door to call Milt, the manager at Chernofski on the lower tip of Unalaska Island. It had successfully operated for many years so maybe someone there could explain what was going on.

Charlie came back shortly and I met him at the back of the class room. He said that after he described the situation, Milt told him that lupine, a purple flower that grows wild in many places in Alaska, contains a chemical that causes paralysis in the spring when it first blossoms. After the first year sheep develop immunity to the toxic chemical in the blossoms and aren't affected by them in the future. The paralysis made the wool-heavy animals fall over. Unable to right themselves they could not get to food or water. We had not heard of this problem with sheep from anyone, and maybe the Choates hadn't run into it. However, the information provided an explanation but it came too late. "Now I gotta get going so I can help Hans with those sheep. We'll probably be over there awhile." I didn't answer him.

I knew we lost a huge investment and I didn't know if Hans and Charlie would hang on. Charlie had been ready to quit after we lost the bull, and in some ways, with his attitude he acted like he had. But Hans kept trying to encourage him, saying things would turn around, the ranch just needed more time—he didn't add 'and money.' After I got over the shock, I began to feel bitter at the turn of events. The whole ranch seemed to be imploding. Why did we ever think we could take on a ranch with no real experience and out on some tiny dot in the North Pacific?

During recess Becky came to me and asked why her dad had come back. I didn't want her to pick up my negative vibes, so I just said they'd lost some sheep but they're taking care of it. Then I told her they'd be busy for a while so it'd just be the three of us for a week or two.

When the guys returned, they told me they estimated the loss at over half the flock. We weren't quite a year into the ranch operation, and our resources were almost drained. Though I would be leaving for Anchorage when classes ended, I still cared about the ranch and hoped they could make something of it. On paper I was still a partner.

A few years before, back in the BLM office in Anchorage, we couldn't know how much land we'd really need. In the early '60s it seemed like there were a lot of islands, mostly uninhabited, available for grazing leases. We chose Akutan Island because it had a village on it, with plane and mail service, even though it was infrequent. We added Akun since it was close to Akutan and thought it would be better to put sheep there without them wandering all over the village. We didn't know they would have been better off on the same island with us. There was a lot we didn't know, since no one had attempted to start a sheep and cattle ranch on Akutan and Akun prior to ours. We knew sheep had been successfully raised at Chernofski for years, and cattle did well on Kodiak, so why wouldn't it work for us? What could go wrong? We never heard any 'failure' stories, only the ones about the ranches that 'made' it. In retrospect, I'm glad because maybe we would have decided against one of the more remarkable experiences of our lives. Sometimes too much information keeps a person from even trying something different.

Later that spring of '66, we were saddened to receive word that Rufus Choate unexpectedly died of a heart attack in Unalaska, just two years after he and his family moved from Montana to start their sheep and cattle ranch. He was only in his mid '50s. His wife, Alice, with the help of her children, planned to continue with their ranch, and didn't seem to have the problems we'd run into, possibly because of more experience and capital. Rufus had been a helpful resource in our set-up. He willingly shared his knowledge with the guys, informing them of the various items they would need to purchase, making arrangements with a Montana stock broker to procure our animals, and leasing the boat to us. We were thankful for the help he had provided, never treating us as competitors, but more like neophytes that he wanted to take under his wing. With all of the problems we had encountered, we had been spared such a heartbreaking loss as that family had to endure.

During that time, Charlie and Hans were over on Akun a lot doing what they could to salvage the sheep operation, while I had my own work to do as the school year came to an end. There were final exams, administrative paperwork, and preparations for eighth grade graduation, which was a big event as it was an important milestone for the children back in 1966. Some of the older people had completed less than eighth grade, mostly due to circumstances. Often schooling wasn't available because they had lived in areas even more isolated than Akutan, or they had to work at an early age to help with the subsistence way of living.

The graduation ceremony for Robert and Eva was well attended. Seating was limited, but like movie night, the children sat on the floor and the adults at the desks, with Robert and Eva up front with me. I gave a speech about their accomplishments and encouraged both to continue their education, though I knew it meant leaving their families at an early age. My school board president also gave a talk congratulating them. I knew their families were proud of them; they had done well in their studies, and also in the help they gave their younger classmates. Akutan had no high school as the population didn't warrant it. Those who completed eighth grade had to go to boarding schools for Alaska Natives or to high schools in other communities where they could stay with relatives. The decision was difficult for both parents and young teenagers. Sometimes the children who went away were just too lonesome and returned to Akutan. In time the high school situation would change, but not that year.

I was proud of the accomplishments of all my students as they had made tremendous progress and it was rewarding to see how quickly they developed a desire to gain more knowledge. I would miss them. Because there were so many and represented all eight grades, that was the last year Akutan Elementary School was a one-teacher school.

I spent my evenings packing up the school apartment so we could be out of there by the end of May. The clothing and personal items for the children and me were headed for Anchorage, and I boxed up Charlie's and Hans' stuff which was headed for the barn. I worked with a heavy heart unable to figure out what went wrong with the ranch and my marriage. There seemed to be a connection, but I didn't know what. I didn't really want to leave the island. I didn't want to move to a big city with no job and two children to support and another one on the way. Because Hans was like a big brother, I could unload my feelings on him sometimes. He tried to reassure me that he would help me financially whenever he could.

"Somehow, dis ranch vill take off, ve just need to give it more time. And you're still a partner," he said with emphasis.

Chapter

11

Retreat to Anchorage

$As\ soon$ as school ended in May, Becky, Malcolm and I departed on the Goose for the tiny community of Cold Bay on the end of the Alaska Peninsula before the start of the Chain. The Goose stayed there when it wasn't making its regular runs to villages without airstrips. Passengers going to other communities on the Chain and the Peninsula, or Anchorage, changed to other Reeve planes at Cold Bay. From Cold Bay, the children and I made the trip to Anchorage on a DC6, a small plane that could tolerate the strong Aleutian winds. I'd had some rough rides, when it bounced up, down, and sideways but kept going forward, until it got us where we wanted to go.

A the plane headed toward Anchorage I felt a growing anticipation about going to the city with its many stores, libraries, hospitals, TV—I could go on and on. I grew up in big cities, so it was nothing new, but it had been a year since I'd experienced the vibrant energy that cities produce.

But I was saddened that I was leaving behind our dream of a ranch that I no longer felt a part of, the people of the village who had been so friendly and inclusive, the isolation with its relaxing slower pace and solitude and even the excitement of the frequent storms. Most of all I was leaving behind a failed marriage with a third child on the way.

After we reached Anchorage, we stayed with Fred and Jeanette Kent, friends from our Dutch Harbor/Unalaska days, while I checked out rentals and used cars. After I purchased a cheap used car, rented an unfurnished apartment and bought furniture, the money I'd saved from teaching was almost gone. There was little left to finance a new addition.

After the children and I were settled, I went to the state employment office, hoping to have something lined up after the baby was born. There wouldn't be any financial help forthcoming from Charlie. Any money from the wool would be set aside for the two lease payments and the agricultural loan. I was on my own. I met with an interviewer who, after looking at my resume', asked how I'd like to do what she did, interview people and find them jobs. I had no idea what triggered that offer. I'd only put down my nursing and teaching experience. I don't think I put down my ranching experience. Why screw up a good resume'? Later I learned the main require-ment for the job was a college degree—in anything—and a willingness to work. She told me to come back after I had my baby and they could put me to work.

My father came from Overland Park, Kansas in August to stay with Becky and Malcolm when I would be in the hospital. I didn't have to ask him twice; he had never been to Alaska and loved to fish. He was barely off the plane when I had to borrow a pole and tackle box from one of my friends. He was gone until late afternoon almost every day. He had a lot of patience, at least when it came to fishing. Thank goodness I went into labor in the evening. Eric, our new addition, was born in late August and my father left shortly after.

But while Dad was there I told him of my situation, the lack of money and the breakup with Charlie. If someone asked me to describe what my father was like I would probably say he was a grouchy cynic, though now that I'm older I've come to realize that describes lots of aging people. So he surprised me by his understanding of both my and Charlie's situation. He felt Charlie's frustrations got the better of him with so many animal losses that also represented a great deal of money for which Charlie had put in hundreds of hours of overtime with Standard Oil, spending very little of it, in order to start the ranch. He had worked hard and saved money, and so had Hans. The losses affected us all, but Dad thought Charlie's behavior sounded more like a depression, though I'd never seen that side of Charlie, as his outward demeanor was more like the 'what, me worry?' kid. Maybe it was just that he could never really open up and express his true feelings. Hans and I were not the type to hide ours, so it was harder to recognize what was happening to Charlie. Dad advised me to hold off on my divorce plans till after I had the baby, that maybe some of my own reactions had something to do with hormone changes. My attorney had told me the same thing but I didn't tell Dad. I might have if he weren't one of those 'I told you so' people.

I didn't communicate with Charlie after Dad left except to send a marine radio message that he had a baby son named Eric, a name we'd agreed upon which seemed like a long time ago.

That fall Becky and Malcolm attended fifth grade and second grade respectively, in walking distance of where we lived. They missed the island and their dad and Hans. They made friends easily and did well in school, but Akutan had spoiled them for city life.

By now my funds were quite low, and without health insurance, I had to come up with the money to make a down payment on my new son, Eric, before collections repossessed him. I showed up at the state employment office when he was only three weeks old, hoping they hadn't forgotten me and would make good on their offer. True to their word, I began a new career as an employment counselor, placing people in jobs.

Meanwhile, back at the ranch, (doesn't that sound pretentious) the shearing had been completed and the bags of wool loaded onto a fishing boat that took the huge bags to Unalaska where they were combined with the Choates' and shipped to the lower '48. Because our flock was so much smaller, the amount of wool was far less than we had calculated when we made our original plans.

Charlie called me by marine radio in September and said he wanted to go to Anchorage to see his new son and see if we could work out our differences. He apologized for his earlier indifferent behavior and said he hadn't signed the divorce papers I'd sent. I said I was glad, that we had to give it another try. If you've ever used a marine radio you know how awkward it feels to say "Over" after you make your comments, especially when you're trying to salvage a relationship.

Charlie took out enough from the wool proceeds for a plane ticket and flew in to Anchorage that fall. The children were happy to see their father after the long absence and once he held his new son he must have had a better sense of what he had almost lost. He was able to pour out his feelings, sharing the burden he'd been carrying around, how he thought his dream of having a ranch was shattered. He admitted that losing the animals was not as traumatic as losing his family. He had always been a family man and had come to realize how he had neglected us. He didn't want a divorce. I did discuss my own frustrations with him, mainly his lack of financial support the previous winter. But if we could talk more openly we both felt we could work things out.

He found temporary work at the Anchorage Airport fueling jet planes, a job he'd done for a few months while waiting to go to Seattle in the spring of '65 to get the boat ready for sailing. His job helped as my paycheck barely covered housing expenses, babysitter for Eric, gas to make the ten mile drive to work, and food. I had made sure there was enough food for Becky and Malcolm and milk for Eric, but I didn't take a lunch to work, just filled up on the free crackers and coffee in their lunch room. Most of the employees left for lunch, so with no one around I put crackers in my pocket and returned to my desk and worked on job files. I was too embarrassed to let them know the financial mess I was in. Once Charlie got a job my diet improved. I'd had my fill of being a single parent trying to be the breadwinner. That experience also helped me to be more tolerant of Charlie's problems (along with my dad's lecture).

Christmas was much less festive than the previous year, but Charlie and I were happier with each other now than we had been last December. Neither of us liked to talk about the ranch much, but we both agreed that it almost destroyed our marriage. I admitted that living on the island meant more to me than having a ranch there and I went along with his and Hans' plans for the adventure and the opportunity to live in a unique place. Charlie said he had put the ranch before everything and when it didn't go as planned he couldn't deal with it. We decided to try and make the ranch work since it was such a big investment and because Hans had his money tied up in it too, and we felt a certain responsibility to him. But we concluded that family came first, and for the sake of our now three children, we would both make an extra effort to provide them with a home where we would try to get along better.

Charlie returned to the island in February and traded places with Hans, to give him a break, plus he also needed to make some money because of the minimal amount the ranch provided. Like Charlie, Hans had not been to town—Anchorage—since we'd landed in Akutan the summer of '65, almost two years before. He had used those long months to complete his GED.

A few years later while on the island he would complete his first college course by correspondence. To improve his mastery of the English language he had signed up for English 101 and intrigued his instructor with essays about the horrors a child experienced growing up in war-torn Germany. Though he made frequent use of a dictionary much of his writings reflected his matter-of-fact blunt personality. Reading them was like hearing him talk, minus the accent.

Upon arriving in Anchorage, he stayed with the three children and me while working at his old job as a union painter for a contractor who did large projects such as groups of buildings all over the state, though Hans only accepted work in Anchorage. He was very fast, and his work was flawless, whether interior or exterior; he was proficient in all phases of the trade, whatever the job demanded, so he was never out of work. His trade school training had paid off, in spite of his unhappiness that his mother had chosen high school for his sister but not for him, a situation that he rectified during his Akutan years.

Before he returned to Akutan that April of '67 to get back on the building projects and help Charlie with the animals, I told him I planned to return there by fall. I considered that adequate notice to have some sort of dwelling available for our return. He tried to discourage me as he informed me they hadn't even started the cabin when he came to town because there had been other work to do. They had just camped out in the barn or in the fishing cabin on Akun. As far as I was concerned, the cabin had now become a priority.

"The barn went up that first summer," I argued, "and there was even more to do then. So a rough cabin shouldn't take more than a few months to construct. I can't afford to stay in town too much longer on just my salary. And these children should be with their father."

"I'm just letting you know. Building a cabin for six people takes a lot longer den a vindowless uninsulated barn," Hans said, defending their actions.

After he left, I started saving ever dollar I could to return to Akutan. I didn't expect any financial help from them—that situation hadn't changed—but I knew what I wanted. I missed the island lifestyle and I missed Charlie's companionship even though he was a different person from the man I married and knew for those first ten years. The ranch losses had left scars that were slow healing. I knew by then I'd have to give him time and a little more understanding if we were going to make it as a family.

Hans and I were strangely not very affected by the ranch problems, though for different reasons. He was able to take it all in and just keep a positive but realistic attitude. I could handle those problems because I knew nothing about ranching and relied solely on Charlie's knowledge and interest. Basically I wanted to live in a small community on an island. Strange as it may seem to some, it had great appeal to me. The ranch was just a means of supporting us, but it could have been something less exotic sounding. Hans and Charlie could have said they wanted to quit their day jobs and live on an island and become fishermen. I would have gone along with that plan, too.

Another advantage of the ranch, though, was that it gave us a chance to own property, a five acre home site, by just proving up on the land and sticking it out for five years. We didn't want to lose our chance at getting some land so the ranch had a certain importance in the overall plan, though that part had relied too heavily on Charlie's limited knowledge. I would try to be more involved and more encouraging if I could just get back there. I was also tired of trying to support myself and three young children on a very small wage working forty hours a week—and I wanted to spend more time to be with my new little son.

I received little word out of Akutan because of the difficult, slow communication, since plane service and radio contact hadn't changed since we arrived in '65. I didn't know what was going on and was getting exasperated. I had my doubts that the cabin was started, though Charlie and Hans knew I hoped to get back there as soon as I had enough money.

Three summers had gone by since we started the ranch, and as a one-third partner, I intended to exercise my right to be a part of the operation. I had gone into it as ill-prepared as Charlie and Hans but had decided to see it through along with them, whatever the outcome. Eric was now a healthy thirteen month old chubby toddler. It was time to get back to Akutan, to go home.

I sent off a marine radio message to Charlie the end of September informing him I had purchased plane tickets and was arriving in Akutan in about a week, weather permitting. Further, all of our belongings, including furniture that I had taken apart bolt by bolt and screw by screw, were boxed and at the post office and would probably arrive on the same plane.

I received a quick radio reply, with frantic overtones, stating, "We aren't ready for you. Wait a bit." I had already done sixteen months of that. The children and I stepped off the Goose a week later.

Chapter

12

Return to Akutan

Charlie was waiting for us on the landing beach in town. He tried to look happy to see us, but I sensed something was wrong. There was a slight frown mixed with his welcoming smile as he reached for Eric. "Hi, kids. Eric, what a big boy you are. My, how you've grown."

Though Charlie was a stranger to him, Eric was very friendly and didn't seem to care when Charlie picked him up. After giving Becky and Malcolm hugs, Charlie turned to me. "I'm glad to see you," he said, which sounded kind of weak. He loaded our stuff into the dory and then sighed, "I wish you would have waited."

I bristled a little. "How much longer?"

He simply said, "Maybe next summer." Somehow this wasn't the happy reunion I'd pictured. He didn't say any more. Then the loud noise of the boat engine made it impossible to talk anyway, without shouting. That would come later.

As we approached the head of the bay I saw a very nice painted structure, though only one. Since it had no windows I knew it was the barn, which had been a bit rougher looking when I left sixteen months before.

I couldn't contain my disappointment. "Where is the cabin?" I shouted over the engine.

Charlie pointed to his right, about fifty feet from the barn and a little further back from the beach. All I saw was some stumps sticking out of the ground.

"That's it?"

I didn't get an answer as Charlie ran the dory up on the beach and I got a clearer picture of the home site area we'd marked off that first summer. I also had a very good view of a first-class barn that was directly in front of us. I knew they had a busy summer and little money to hire extra help. Returning to Akutan may have been a mistake but I wanted so much to get back and so did Becky and Malcolm. I ignored the possibility we might be returning to more primitive conditions than Uncle Paul's cabin, but being crowded in the barn might be the incentive needed to accelerate the building program. I wanted to make our marriage work and was trying to understand what Charlie had gone through with the downward turn of the ranch, but I also felt responsible for seeing that our three children were provided with a home. From his defensive attitude I think he felt guilty that he and Hans hadn't got anything done on the cabin. I knew he was genuinely glad to be reunited with the four of us though; it had been eight months.

Hans came down to the boat to greet us and help unload. Becky and Malcolm jumped onto the beach yelling happily as they ran to him. "Hansie! Hansie!" It seemed they were all over him as he gathered them up, smiling. Where Charlie seemed somewhat reserved around his children, Hans was very demonstrative, lavish in affection and blunt-spoken in his discipline. They loved their Uncle Hansie, I think as much as they loved their parents. He had been a part of our family for four years already. A confirmed bachelor, he had no children of his own. In adopting mine in his heart, they were blessed with having three loving, caring parents. He deserved a lot of credit for how well all the children turned out.

We piled our boxes in the front part of the barn, and I knew many would remain packed till the cabin was built. While the barn was fairly large, the majority of the space was filled. There were no windows and the only ventilation or view outside the barn was a small hole somewhat low in the door. One had to bend over before peering out—which was more like squinting, the hole was so small—but first a stapled piece of pasteboard had to be lifted or removed. It was kept in place to keep out the cold air when there wasn't a need to see outside.

That afternoon the guys quickly threw together a few more bunks consisting of two by fours for legs and frames plus attached sheets of plywood, along the side walls near the front. They placed cotton mattresses, probably no more than two inches thick, on the plywood, which made for pretty firm (translation: hard) beds, but surprisingly we got used to them. The children and I explored outside while they worked. There were so many other inconveniences of a more serious nature that challenged our ability to adjust. With no indoor plumbing, no running water, no electricity and only limited light provided by Coleman lanterns, I thought kind thoughts about Uncle Paul's cabin with its cold water tap and bucket-flushed toilet.

Charlie came outside. "Okay, the bunks are finished. Sorry we hadn't done them yet. I just didn't believe you'd really come back without the cabin built."

"I told you I'd be on that plane. You should know me by now."

"Well, I'm glad you came. I mean it. So much hasn't gone right. I've missed out so much on the kids, but maybe we can still make a go of it. It's going to be rough for a bit, but it'll work."

We went back inside and I got a few things unpacked—not much, as bales of hay and sacks of feed took priority. We would probably be living out of suitcases and boxes for a month or two.

The oil cook stove that also provided our heat was in the center of the limited front space and always on now that the damp chill of the Aleutian fall was in full swing.

As for the plumbing situation, all our water came from the nearby creek, which was narrow and swift moving, fed from the hillside about three-fourths of a mile from our barn. The bathroom consisted of a plywood structure covering a hole in the ground, close to the barn. Calling it a structure is misleading; three pieces of plywood formed the sides and back and a scrap covered the top to keep the rain out. The door was another sheet of plywood just leaning against the opening. I had mixed feelings about the cabin they were going to build.

Before leaving Anchorage, I had requested that the Department of Education send correspondence courses to Akutan so I could home school Becky and Malcolm for that school year. Alaska provided this service for the many children living in the Bush as there were small pockets of families all over the huge state, living in various remote areas with not enough children for the state to provide a school. The two teachers at the Akutan School that year—yes, two the year after I taught, though the enrollment was the same—loaned Charlie two school desks, which we crowded into the limited floor space of our barn/home. On the next plane after our arrival their course materials showed up from Juneau.

By the limited light of a Coleman lantern, in a crowded cold room smelling of hay and stove oil, Becky and Malcolm continued their studies. Their classroom situation had reached a new low. When they were grown, and listened to others who grew up in the Bush talk about their one room school experiences, those two could easily top them with, "Yes, well I went to school in a hay barn with no windows, lit only by lanterns and barely enough room for my desk—at least for a few months." I am not an advocate of holding classes in hay barns, so in order to avoid my comments regarding that situation Charlie and Hans were out of the barn early every morning, rain or shine, and put in long hours at the construction area.

The cabin site was not far from the barn and situated about a hundred feet from the bay in a fairly dry level area that sloped gently toward the beach where quite a bit of gray sand was visible, even at high tide. The minus tides graphically revealed how shallow the water was in that area, as mud flats stretched very far out into the bay. For that reason, the larger boats anchored a long way from shore when they brought supplies to us, such as barrels of oil and bags of food. The guys had to take off in the dory on high tide, and then make it back with the supplies before the tide started back out.

The valley behind our site had a prairie-like appearance with its tall rye grass, scrubby blueberry bushes, wild lupine, and absence of trees. This misleading appearance hid the swamp that covered much of the terrain, often with ankle-deep water. Small hummocks of spongy moss with tiny dark berries made walking somewhat difficult as our feet would sink down into the water, so rubber boots were the standard footwear.

Three creeks flowed from the base of the surrounding hills and snaked across the land, then emptied into the bay. We called the nearest Third Creek. About fifty feet from our cabin site, it became our only source of water for over a year. Shallow, narrow and swift-running, it was clear and cold.

The building project above those stumps began to move at an accelerated pace though we didn't have a generator yet so they didn't have the advantage of the use of power tools to speed up the process. By November they still had a lot to do, though we hoped to move in before Christmas. When the three children didn't need my supervision, I helped pound nails, while bundled up against the cold late fall winds, as I knew they could use the extra help. Charlie and Hans still had their day to day animal chores, which took up a certain amount of time.

One unfortunate event occurred during that time when a bull calf got stuck in the thick, swamp-like mud in the middle of the creek farthest from our cabin, on the town side. The creek was the largest of those that formed across the flat land at the foot of the surrounding hills. We normally walked down to the beach when we got close to it and waded through the rivulets of creek water till we got around it as the land surrounding it was boggy, and the creek itself was more of a swamp.

That poor bull for some reason tried to walk straight across it and the inevitable happened as it reached the middle and could no longer go further, could not lift its legs.

"What's that loud noise, Mama?" Malcolm asked as he looked up from his desk. Becky and I heard it, too. We all went outside and saw the tragic scene in the distance. The guys were already outside and Charlie was running toward us.

"What happened?" I asked.

"Gotta get some rope. That bull's stuck in the swamp. Hans and I can't reach her. The mud's so thick it's dangerous to walk on." He hurried from the barn as he explained the situation. Then the children and I headed toward that creek and I kept a tight hold on Eric's hand, though we only went close enough to see what was happening.

The miserable bull's loud mooing sounds kept up, while the guys got as close as they dared, hindered by the soft mud, and managed to get the rope on it. But no matter how hard they pulled, it was to no avail, as the bull was too heavy and already too deep into the thick sucking mass. The animal went over on its side and sunk under the water. The children and I remained at a distance and I was reminded of the time I helped Tommy and Ignaty deliver a stillborn calf a few years ago. I thought how much worse it could have been if that pregnant cow had headed into the swampy creek in her misery. The children had already been warned to stay away from that dangerous area, to go down to the beach to get around it, and after witnessing that sad and frightening scene, they didn't need to be reminded to avoid it. I hurried them back to the barn, not wanting to spend any more time dwelling on that traumatic event. That young bull was one of Duke's replacements, probably inherited some of the 'stupid' genes.

In our limited living quarters, one would think there wasn't much Eric could get into. But at fifteen months he was curious about everything no matter what it was or where it was. He also pretended not to have mastered enough of the English language to understand basic commands. He was all over the crowded barn and explored everything. One of his more memorable explorations involved the pasteboard stapled over the hole in the door. He was just tall enough to pull the bottom loose so he could look out the small hole. One day, as he pressed his face against the hole to see out, we heard a loud scream. Eric turned around and blood was dripping down his chin from a large deep cut on his upper lip. A staple (the heavy duty variety) had one end sticking out and had snagged Eric's lip. The blood made it look worse than it was and I was able to stop it with pressure and made him a fancy bandage from my medical kit. He ended up with a permanent scar where his lip was ripped open. While it didn't mar his appearance, it provided an opportunity for him to explain a rather unique way of acquiring it.

Charlie and I were getting along pretty good working on the cabin together. He was a good carpenter, having taught shop at Seward High School when we first came to Alaska in '58. I was able to do the tasks that didn't require too much muscle, and found I enjoyed it. When I wasn't busy in the barn I was over at the site willing to help, as I tried to speed things along.

One sunny, calm day Hans went to Akun to check on the sheep that remained there. Charlie decided to take advantage of the break in the weather to put the roll roofing on the cabin and get it covered before the snow came. It's a two person job, so I was that second person, up on the roof helping him when a skiff pulled up on the beach. Peter Stepetin climbed out and headed toward the cabin. He yelled up at me, "Get down from there! That's not woman's work. I'll help Charlie."

I took no offense and was in fact, happy to oblige. I've never liked heights. It was sheer necessity that got me up there. So generous with his time, Peter, like the other villagers, wouldn't take compensation, just wanted to help. With the extra help some of them provided occasionally, I was encouraged to believe that we wouldn't have to spend Christmas in the barn.

13

Cabin in the Valley

Late afternoon in early December, just after darkness set in, Charlie and Hans returned to the barn after working on the cabin during the limited daylight hours. As Charlie approached the oil stove to warm his hands, he announced, "Tomorrow is moving day. We still got a lot to do but it'll be better than this."

There was no argument from me. I had waited for that day for two and a half years. "Yeah, it's about time. We need to get at some of our stuff, and it'll be good to have more floor space."

"We can get the stove over there after we turn it off and let it cool down," Charlie said. "While we're waiting we can get the boxes and beds moved."

Now that the reality of it was setting in, was it worth the wait? I wanted to believe that it was. Though still in its shell stage, the cabin would be our first real home here, one that was our own. After the problems Charlie and I went through, I hoped the cabin would at least symbolically bring us closer. Time would tell.

I wouldn't miss the musty hay smell, plus the new building had a real window and faced the bay, so we would have more than a bird's eye view when we looked out. The cabin was 16X28 with plywood floors and walls.

Though the partitions and insulation weren't in yet, it would be quicker and easier to do the inside work now that we were 'living on the job.' All of us were excited about the move, which was one of the more positive milestones in our ranch operation.

There was a lot more floor space, which we quickly filled with our boxes and the reassembled furniture I'd shipped from Anchorage. We arranged the plywood beds with their 2X4 legs against the walls during the day to double as places to sit, and at night slid them close to the stove. Becky and Malcolm placed their school desks near the front window to take advantage of the limited winter daylight as we had no electricity, and relied on the two Coleman gas lanterns for light in the evening.

Sugar and Malt had shared a small corner of the crowded barn with us, so they now shared in the roomier quarters of the cabin, though they spent their days roaming the hills in search of foxes when they weren't stretched out on the plywood deck by the door.

Till we could get some partitions up we made a wall of blankets to seal off part of the cabin so that we could have more light and heat in the living area. We used the dark cold room for storage.

I've described the barn door as an old weathered relic. That didn't do it justice. That door was far superior to the piece of plywood on hinges that served as the cabin door, with its outside lock just a padlock on a hasp. In order to keep the 'door' shut while we were inside, a small rectangular block of wood with a nail running through it and into the stud alongside the door had to be turned sideways to hold the door shut. Not one of the better examples of Charlie's carpenter skills, but that little block of wood kept the wind out.

We ordered foil backed insulation rolls and ceiling panels made of material called Cellotex, from the Sears catalog, our mainstay in those days for most of what we needed. When the materials arrived, we piled them in the dark cold half of the cabin. Once we were sufficiently settled in, Charlie and Hans put up 2 X 4 partitions and hung the ceiling panels. I cut and stapled the insulation on all the walls, which stopped a lot of air leaks and gave the main room a shiny look as the lantern light reflected off the silver foil. Plywood was at a premium so we would have those aluminum covered walls for quite a while. Our cabin rapidly got warmer as the three of us worked long hours, now that we were in it all the time.

When the framework for the partitions was up we took down the blankets and put them on our narrow wooden beds. We replaced them with large sheets of cardboard stapled to the dividing frames. Eric could write on the walls to his heart's content and not have his artistic abilities stunted at that formative age. Though we had only a little more floor space in that heated room, I felt the atmosphere was much homier than the barn.

We partially covered the bare floor with an assortment of small rectangular carpet samples in a variety of colors, patterns and materials, which made it softer and warmer. I had purchased discounted samples from a carpet store in Anchorage and brought them with me. We now had a multicolored patchwork quilt rug that fit right in with the rest of the décor.

Living without modern conveniences, everybody had chores. While Charlie and Hans worked on the inside of the cabin, Becky and Malcolm provided our water supply. They took buckets to the creek every day and filled them, then hauled them back to the cabin where each filled a tub. It took quite a few trips, especially for Malcolm as he was only eight and the buckets were heavy. He couldn't fill his as full as Becky and sometimes he spilled some of the water. He wasn't happy about making extra trips but he always did his share.

We used the creek water for everything, cooking, drinking, cleaning, washing dishes and clothes, and bathing in the proverbial round galvanized tub. None of us ever got sick from the water or anything else while we lived there. I brought a few medical supplies back with me but never needed more than a band aid or aspirin. I have no explanation other than hard work and no fast food or tobacco. Our immune systems seemed to work very well. We also had the advantage of clean, unpolluted air.

Without a washing machine, I washed clothes for the six of us in a large tub filled with water heated on the oil stove. The agitator was a large stick. I soaked the clothes for a few hours, and gave them a stir with the stick between doing other chores. With Eric still in diapers, the old fashioned kind, I stirred something in the tub almost every day.

Because of the normally inclement weather, there were permanent clotheslines strung up in the cabin and something always hung on them, diapers if nothing else. Charlie had put up outside clotheslines also, but they were only good on dry days in the summer. They didn't get a lot of use.

Becky and Malcolm spent much of their time working on schoolwork, but they had occasional distractions. Since our cabin was close to the beach we could hear the waves as they pounded the shore, and the frequent storms brought sheets of rain that pelted our front window with bullet-like sounds driven by gusts that could have been up to one hundred miles an hour, or so it seemed. The children sometimes left their desks to stare out the window in fascination at the crashing roaring mountains of water in the eerie semi-darkness.

On the infrequent sunny days, Becky asked, "Can we play outside? We can do our assignments in the evening." I usually let them and they needed the fresh air and exercise, so I wanted them to take advantage of it.

"Take Eric with you. You know how he likes to try and explore the beaches on his own. Keep a close eye on him."

After we were settled in the cabin that December, I ordered one hundred Rhode Island Red mixed run 'day old' chicks from a Washington hatchery. They were flown to Anchorage, a three or four hour flight, and then placed on the DC-3 to Cold Bay, another hour of flying time. They would be placed on the Goose on its scheduled day, for the final leg. We expected the inevitable weather delays and weren't disappointed. Two weeks after leaving Cold Bay, just a hundred miles away, the plane made it in. By then some of the chicks had little brown feathers sprouting on their soft yellow bodies. I was grateful to the people at Cold Bay who fed, watered and kept them warm the whole time, and at no additional cost to us –neighborliness was common in those days. Though a few of the chickens were lost, mostly due to crowding when they huddled in corners, the great majority made the long journey just fine and looked pretty good. I had high hopes for this new undertaking.

In our main room, the heated one, Charlie built an eight foot square plywood brooder and placed it three feet off the floor on two by four legs. Besides putting it close to the stove, Charlie placed one of the two Coleman

Our first winter in the cabin, Eric is next to our second-hand oil stove that provided our heat and was great for baking and keeping the always-filled teapot hot.

lanterns under it for additional heat. Those little chicks were warmer than we were when the cold January winds blew. We spent a lot of time separating them as they still liked to huddle, but there were dividers in the brooder so they were in fairly small groups. We dispensed with the lantern under the brooder as they got more of their feathers, but not before Eric was able to crawl up to it and check it out, though we had tried to teach him words like 'no' and 'don't.' He was literally a hands-on kind of child. One day I observed him as he crawled toward the lantern.

"Hot! No! Eric, get back here! Right now!"

As usual, he pretended not to hear me or understand me, or both. Just as I reached under to pull him out, he let out a yell. He had put his hand on the lantern and ended up with yet another small permanent scar. He was beginning to grasp the English language.

Unlike Eric, Sugar and Malt showed little interest in the new additions, apparently accepting them as creatures the humans seemed to care about.

The chickens thrived with all the attention they were getting, located in the heart of our living space, but they soon outgrew their cramped quarters—getting so big that they had little room to move in that brooder. It was a happy day for all of us when, much to our relief, Charlie announced, "We're getting those damn chickens out of here today."

There was a resounding chorus of, "Yay!" They had overstayed their welcome and it was time for them to move on, at least to the other side of the cardboard wall. We all sprang into action. Charlie had closed off a portion of the back room and put down newspapers and straw, in anticipation of this day. Now he took one of the lanterns and hung it overhead in their new quarters so they would have heat and light. I would still have to do my night reading by flashlight, which was a little cumbersome, but the inconvenience was worth it.

One advantage—I could move my homemade bunk closer to the stove, now that those creatures weren't hogging so much of the limited heat. But I still had to try and sleep through their constant peeping and squawking—and did I mention the smell?

I felt a little resentful of their presence, along with the inconvenience and extra work for me, but I wouldn't complain as it had been my idea, and the children were quite happy to have so many pets. The chickens acted quite tame, probably enjoying all the attention from the three children. Maybe they considered themselves part of our family, living in such close proximity to us. As chickens go, Rhode Island Reds are a fairly large breed, so they quickly filled their newly allotted space. I observed their rapid growth almost daily, like the witch in *Hansel and Gretel*, though I didn't plan to eat them—at least not right way. I began to wonder if they lived in my house or I lived in a chicken house.

Charlie and Hans built a small chicken coop near the barn complete with nests and roosts, but it had no heat, so we had to wait till the chickens were full grown. I felt that shouldn't take long, at the rate they devoured their feed.

One morning I made the decision. "I think they've done growing. I don't care what plans any of you have. Grab a chicken and help me get these foul creatures out of here."

Again, no one needed any encouragement. I'm sure their thoughts were similar to mine. We carried those large brown birds out of there and down to their latest home, one at a time, which made for lots of trips, though no one complained. Those creatures had pretty much taken over the cabin with their noise and their smell. We left our plywood door open while we made those many trips in order to air out the cabin. That night it was so quiet I had trouble getting to sleep at first, but got over that rather quickly.

The guys didn't fence in a 'run' because we wanted the chickens to roam outside at will, but kept feed and water available in their shelter. They always went in at night to roost and one of us closed the door, then opened it in the morning. They didn't need as much store-bought feed that way, but there was a drawback. Not all of the hens laid their eggs in the built-in nests; some found it more convenient to leave them in the tall grasses. Gathering the eggs was one of the children's jobs, and that chore turned into a genuine Easter egg-style hunt—every day.

One hen picked her own spot outside in the high grass where she deposited her almost daily egg. Becky and Malcolm felt sorry for her because of the weather; that is, rainy, stormy, foggy, windy—nothing out of the ordinary. The children used two scraps of lumber about 8 inches by 11 inches and built her a shelter against the hummock where she chose to lay her eggs. They still cared about their former house pets, so I didn't have the heart to tell them that the nonproducers, the ones growing rather large combs, were headed for the frying pan.

Now that our cabin was quieter, and we again had the use of the second lantern, we enjoyed reading during our long winter evenings. We always had a large supply of books on hand as we received a varied assortment from the state lending library out of Juneau once a month. Though they chose the books, we received some great selections. Also, the fishing boats traded boxes of paperbacks for eggs or chickens. When we were done reading the boat books, we traded boxes of them to other boats in exchange for fuel for our stove, so it worked out well for everyone. I was not a fan of fantasy literature, but desperate for something to read, as I awaited a new book supply, I was introduced to J.R.R. Tolkien's *The Lord of the Rings.* That book made me an instant fan of his, and a latter day (occasional) fantasy reader. Of course, once the weather improved a lot of our reading time would be greatly curtailed.

During the limited daylight hours, I sometimes took breaks to do my other favorite recreational activity, oil painting, which required more light than the Colemans provided. I mostly did landscapes and one was a 20X24 inch painting of what was called the whaling station, an old abandoned dock and storage tanks that were part of a long ago operation at Akutan. I could see the place from our front window as it was only about a quarter mile away. Almost fifty years later that reminder of another time still hangs on my wall depicting an historical sight that had been there since the early nineteen hundreds, but didn't survive the advancement of civilization.

Sometimes villagers came by boat to visit and see how we were coming along with our new living quarters. Though the place was still in an unfinished state, it was fun to have company and serve tea while they sat on one of our rather hard plywood 'couches.' No one ever visited me in the barn, so that was kind of lonely, but it was just as well I was spared the embarrassment of having them see those living conditions. I probably should have felt a little embarrassed about the cabin. No dwelling in the village was as primitive as ours, but I was actually kind of proud of it since the three of us had built it ourselves, which made it special to me. I looked forward to the visits and didn't feel I had to apologize for the strings of clothesline that were permanent fixtures overhead, the noisy chickens that lived with us for a while, etc. Maybe they just thought we were part of the 60's hippie culture, though I'm not sure they had much knowledge of it back then. In our isolation we didn't either, so maybe we were and didn't know it.

Though we no longer enjoyed many modern-day comforts and were living in substandard conditions, Charlie and I grew closer as a couple. Our present life was more what we'd envisioned when we took on this Akutan adventure. Finally, it was happening.

Chapter

14

Pigs, Whales, and MLK

Since the poultry venture was meeting with more success than the sheep and cattle venture, in the early spring of '68 we decided to expand our ranching efforts and try our hand at pig farming. The Choates at Unalaska raised hogs on their ranch so Charlie and Hans went over on a fishing boat one day to see about purchasing some. They returned the next day with an adult boar and two huge pink pregnant sows. The plan was to offload them onto the village skiff and take them to the head of the bay.

All went well with the huge cumbersome sows, but when the time came to load the boar into the skiff, it balked at the idea and took everyone by surprise when it leaped into the bay, then headed directly for the far shore, almost two miles away. The guys plus several villagers got in the skiff and chased the runaway, looking like cowboys trying to catch a wild horse, as they wielded a lasso in the air. After quite a struggle, before the boar reached the other side, they got the lasso around it and pulled the elusive pig into the skiff. As they returned to the village shore to pick up the kids and me, all the villagers standing on the beach cheered the marine hog wranglers. As always, with any unusual event, the community turned out, some to observe, and others to offer assistance.

Our joy was short lived. As soon as the lasso was removed the men tried unsuccessfully to get a handhold on the animal but the huge round boar didn't have much to grab onto. In the midst of the struggle, it jumped back into the water. I'd never known pigs could swim so fast, if at all, and this time it was headed for the open water toward the entrance to the bay, in the direction of Akun. Several skiffs that had been standing by also joined in hot pursuit, but the animal had already expended an excessive amount of energy. Just as they approached the boar, his head dipped below the surface and did not reappear. As with some of our other ranch ventures, this one did not start out well.

At least the sows were already impregnated, and they seemed to have no thoughts of swimming in those icy, turbulent waters. We hauled them to the head of the bay without incident.

One of the two sows had no ears as a dog back in Unalaska had bitten them off. She looked like a giant well-fed rat with her sloping head and long thin tail. We named her Slick Pig. Despite her traumatic experience with a dog, she was quite friendly and often came up to us making snorting sounds, as she looked up with an expression that was a cross between curiosity and a desire to communicate. I liked being around her.

The other pig earned the name Fish Head after she gobbled up a halibut someone had given us. We had left it on the stained plywood deck in front of the cabin, waiting to be cleaned later. Besides being a thief, she was quite unfriendly and unapproachable. When she looked at me with beady eyes, always from a distance, I interpreted it as mean. Maybe she was still mad at me for yelling at her when I caught her eating our dinner.

The guys built a pen and small shelter for the two sows near the chicken house and barn. Our front yard was beginning to take on the appearance of an animal motel. Once the sows became used to being fed in their pen, we left it open and they became range pigs. Slick and Fish Head roamed and rooted around all day but they never strayed far as we gave them pig mash in their pen every evening.

I forgot that hogs were rooting animals when I dug about ten holes in front of our cabin and planted some potatoes that spring. Since the soil wasn't very good I threw a little fish meal in each hole for fertilizer. The

In the spring of '68 Fishhead produced thirteen piglets in a variety of colors and patterns, from solid browns and blacks to multicolored spots. They were so small they looked like children's plush dolls and just as cute. Fishhead didn't mellow with motherhood, though. If anything, her disposition seemed meaner.

next day I had two happy pigs and ten empty holes. I wonder if they were annoyed that I had put dirt on their food—not very thoughtful of me. With those two around all the time, I made no further attempts at gardening. Later that summer, I stopped begrudging Slick and Fish Head for putting a swift end to my attempts when they went into the pork production business big time. But that came later.

In the meantime, Becky and Malcolm continued working on their correspondence courses for the sixth and third grades, respectively. They took the courses seriously and made good progress, though sometimes they were at their desks till late in the evening. No, they weren't that studious; they had to make up for various distractions that took them away from their schoolwork during the day.

Besides storm watching at the front window and going outside on the rare sunny days, they also found another excuse to jump up from their desks and run to the front window. The huge gray whales returned to Akutan

Bay, which they did every spring as it was in their migration path. Those sea monsters were suddenly everywhere, leaping in the air, then diving and spouting, sometimes several of them at a time. We had our own private sea life show, more spectacular than any performance a viewer would have to pay to see at a marine park. The distraction delayed the schoolwork even more, as my two students spent lots of time watching the show. I couldn't reprimand them since I was right there with them, holding up Eric, while all of us watched the return of the whales.

When they did get free time to go outside and play, one of their activities peculiar to the area—maybe just to them- was to run down to the beach, right into williwaws (sudden violent squalls) with their eyes closed as the winds encircled them, pelting them with dry sand and sea weed from the beach. These were the days before electronic entertainment replaced nature for ways to amuse children.

On a dark, misty evening in April we received news that brought home to us how provincial life was in 1968 Akutan. Isolated from the rest of the world, with limited forms of communication, we had become oblivious to events happening outside our immediate surroundings. We heard a boat engine, and spotted a small skiff approaching our beach. A short time later we recognized the local school teacher, Steve Grubis, as he walked toward our cabin. It was unusual for him to visit us, especially late in the day. After he entered and warmed himself by the oil cook stove, Charlie asked what brought him out.

Steve said, "I just had to tell somebody."

As he paused, Charlie asked, "What? What happened?"

He exclaimed, "I just found out Martin Luther King has been assassinated! When I heard the news on the short wave, I rushed out and told the first couple of villagers I came across. Only one person responded. He asked, 'What boat was he on?' "

I mentioned earlier a painting I did of an abandoned whaling station on the island. It was located about a quarter of a mile from us along the beach on the opposite side of the bay from the village. The old whaling station had closed its operation in 1942, right after the start of WWII, after thirty years in operation. The rotting dock had holes big enough for a man's

A whale is spouting near the head of the bay. We watched amazing sea-life shows every summer as the huge whales performed for us before continuing on their migratory path.

foot and in some places entire planks were gone. Many of the old pilings were busted and caused one end of the long dock to sag sharply. Three massive storage tanks still stood. While the children and I were in Anchorage that second year, Charlie and Hans discovered a small abandoned bath house—banya- in disrepair near the deteriorating dock. At first it had looked like a gray weathered shed, but when they realized what it was, they brought it back into useable condition. It was quite a find for two big guys, each over two hundred pounds, as they hadn't liked attempting to clean themselves in our small galvanized tub. Occasionally, the children and I went for a steam bath, but I still preferred the round metal tub in the warm cabin to the walk back from the banya along the windy beach, shivering, with my hair wet and my skin damp. I was a small person so I could more easily make do with the little tub, but I was happy for the guys.

Another of our primitive problems was solved when two village men came to our cabin that late spring. We were just getting ready for dinner when we heard the engine. When we looked out the door, Ignaty and Tommy had just pulled up on the beach, the same two who had helped with the calf delivery two years previously.

Charlie shouted, "Hi, guys. Come on up. What's happening?"

Tommy yelled, "We brought you a present."

Charlie went back inside and we wondered what they had brought. Over the months we were the recipients of many presents from the villagers, from sea lion liver to blueberry jam. When Tommy and Ignaty entered, they just stood in the doorway and weren't holding anything.

Tommy said, "We brought you something if you want it. Irene and I bought a new washing machine, but the old one works okay. We just wanted a more modern one. We thought maybe you guys would like the old one since you picked up that second-hand Onan."

I'm sure his wife, Irene, had contributed to the discussion as she was also aware of our situation and had always been very friendly to me when I lived in the village. She was the sister of the young mother that had lost her daughter the day we had arrived in Akutan.

He made no reference to my limited laundry facilities, a tub and a stick, which he and Ignaty must have observed when they stopped in to visit at various times while out duck hunting. And he knew we would be able to use the washer since we had bought a small used generator that we only used when absolutely necessary, in order to save on fuel.

Washing clothes consumed much of my time and that would be a great use of the generator, as far as I was concerned. The little tub with water and dirty clothes in it seemed like a permanent fixture in our limited quarters. Finally that came to an end, thanks to Tommy's thoughtfulness. Most of the people of Akutan were aware of the difficulties we were facing, both with the ranch and our living conditions and tried to help us whenever possible, often in subtle ways.

Charlie and Hans went back to the boat with our benefactors and helped them bring the washer to the cabin. The twentieth century was catching up with us. I could retire my primitive agitator (stick).

Because of the limited mail service, weeks usually went by between Becky and Malcolm sending their lessons to Juneau and receiving them back some weeks later. Because of those delays plus the earlier mentioned distractions, it was sometime in June before they finished their courses. They weren't happy about losing part of their summer confined to desks; fall starts early at Akutan. However, they had one less chore that summer.

Charlie and Hans obtained large coils of rubber hose and connected them together, then anchored one end to a waterfall on the hillside to divert some of the water into it. The black tubing stretched across the flat swampland for almost a quarter of a mile like an extremely long skinny snake, though it was barely visible through the tall wild grass, ending at the back wall of our cabin. Charlie set up a small plywood platform against the back wall and cut a hole for a small sink we'd ordered from the Sears catalog. After the hose was inserted through the wall and connected to the plumbing, I had fresh cold mountain water whenever I turned on the faucet, a luxury I'd previously taken for granted most of my life. While I was happy to have the convenience of running water in our house and not have to deal with buckets of creek water, Becky and Malcolm were overjoyed. Our living conditions were showing signs of improvement.

15

Land Freeze

Because of our isolation and limited knowledge of anything that happened outside our little island, we were unaware till the late winter of 1968 that a bill in Congress could have a huge impact on all our plans.

Back in the fall of '66 while the children and I were in Anchorage, Charlie and Hans had marked off five acres at the head of the bay, filled out the required forms and mailed them to the Bureau of Land Management (BLM) for approval of a home site patent.

Under the Homestead Act, to receive the patent, a person had to put an improvement, such as a simple structure, on a five acre parcel and live on the land for three years out of five, which for us meant remaining there till 1971 before becoming eligible to receive the patent.

Unknown to us, while we waited for a response to our request, the Alaska Federation of Natives, AFN, which emerged coincidentally in 1966, worked successfully to halt the disposition of Alaska land while Congress determined their rights to it. Secretary of the Interior Udall ordered the BLM in December of '66 to cease granting patents to lands that the native people were also claiming, until the matter was settled. His order became known as the 'land freeze.'

We eventually received a response to our application from BLM by way of the bi-monthly mail service in early '68, when they informed us of the land freeze, and that no sites were being granted pending the outcome of the Alaska Natives' claims. That was the first we knew about it. I don't know why Charlie and Hans couldn't get that information sooner. I would guess our application languished in some file awaiting the court results and no one kept us informed. The far reaching event had already been common knowledge in some areas of the lower '48, but for us, with no background information or warning signs we couldn't quite comprehend the magnitude of its implications.

Charlie and Hans asked some of the people in the village about it, but because they were also uninformed about many things that occurred beyond the island, they knew little and could shed no new light. A few had heard about the formation of the AFN and said that everyone in the village needed to register and have some sort of proof that they were at least one fourth Alaska Native.

We wrote back to BLM and inquired about our options and were informed, again by slow mail, that we could wait it out, though it might take years. The BLM was fairly certain that if the AFN prevailed, they would claim the land of our requested home site because of its proximity to the Native Reserve, the Akutan village. Also, they wrote that the grazing lands on Akutan and Akun would probably be claimed. If the AFN lost their case, however, we would still have to remain the three years out of five to receive a patent.

As we continued to monitor events in Washington as best we could from our remote area, it appeared to be a very strong claim with lots of support. We never opposed the natives' rights to their claims, but were unhappy with the lack of communication from the BLM. It would seem logical that someone in that department had to have some knowledge of the potential threat to the federal government's Homestead Act regarding Alaska, which that department managed.

Had we known back in '64 that those storm clouds were looming, Charlie, Hans, and I probably would not have sunk our entire life's savings into such a venture, nor would we have taken on the responsibility of an agricultural loan. But we had no inkling of what would occur a few years later. Now we found ourselves caught in the conflict. Perhaps the BLM didn't give the Native land rights claim serious consideration, or maybe the staff in Anchorage had little knowledge that some native leaders, especially those who had become well-educated attorneys, were considering taking on the federal government. These were the days of limited communication in and out of Alaska, long before the electronics revolution, with its computers, fax machines, and cell phones.

The newly formed AFN believed they had aboriginal rights to the land when Russia sold it out from under them to the US. Countries didn't bother with title searches in claiming ownership to vast areas of land; a show of force and planting a flag was sufficient. Russia's claim was just another example of ownership by conquest. After the US purchased the land, some of which rightfully belonged to the native occupants, free required public education was one benefit provided to the already existing inhabitants. In a remarkable use of that benefit, some of the natives became well-educated and began a legal process to reclaim what they considered was rightfully theirs in the first place. What a novel idea, considering the bloody history of land acquisitions world-wide over the centuries.

As the legal battle in Washington picked up strength, our prospects of ever being more than tenants on the land didn't look good. Again we inquired about our situation as we had to decide whether to bring in more stock or just pull out.

The BLM let us know that if the AFN won their suit, our annual grazing lease for all of Akun and about half of Akutan would terminate and we would be required to renegotiate a lease with the Aleut Corporation, which would include far more people than the local villagers who were our friends and had made us feel very welcome. To be a member of the Corporation one only had to provide evidence of one quarter Native blood and could be living anywhere in Alaska, or the US for that matter. The Corporation would have the right to reject our request, or set its own fees and requirements and, according to proposed stipulations, they would not be permitted to sell us the land for many years. Our current fees were extremely reasonable, but our contact at BLM thought it probable that the new fees would be at least triple and for a shorter time period. That prediction was understandable as the federal government had a different agenda when they originally enacted the Homestead Act.

"Well, I think it's time to scale back our operation," Charlie said as he sat at our small table after we had just received the latest information on the land claims by mail. "We don't have the money or the stock to keep up the lease on Akun, so maybe we should bring those remaining sheep over here after shearing?"

"Good idea, Charlie. Ve gottta do someting," Hans responded, and gave no argument; nor did I. I think we knew this day was coming, but none of us had wanted to bring it up. Now it was out in the open. I thought for some time that we were paying for more grazing land than we needed, but I didn't think I should be the one to make the suggestion. Charlie and Hans had put so much time and work into Akun, I knew it would really hurt them to give it up. Now that everything was in a state of flux it was time for some hard decisions, which we had been avoiding. I was glad the suggestion came from Charlie.

"Okay, then. It's settled," Charlie said. "I'll get off a letter to BLM informing them of our intention to cancel our grazing lease on Akun and move our flock to Akutan, and let them know we want to continue the Akutan lease for now."

While awaiting the outcome of the lawsuit and our fate we decided to remain at the head of the bay and just continue with the ranch. At the moment we weren't ready to speculate what we would do if the Claims did go through. But after three years, in that late spring of '68, we gave up the lease on Akun. It had been difficult meeting the lease fees of both islands, plus traveling between the two. Charlie and Hans fenced off a large area behind our cabin, some of which was still standing in 2001 when Doug, my present husband, was on the island. The guys spent a lot of time on Akun as they rounded up, sheared, and transported skiff loads of sheep eight miles to their new home at the head of the bay. They used the village's large wooden seine skiff so they could limit the number of trips. It took quite a bit of their time since they had to depend on getting through the pass with their large loads when the weather was relatively calm.

The children and I enjoyed having those sheep in our back yard. After they became used to their new home we opened their gate during the day so they could have access to more grazing. Then we put feed inside the fence in the evening so the sheep would go back inside. We never had a problem with foxes though we saw them occasionally off in a distance on the hillside. Sugar and Malt always saw them first and were off and running, not to chase them away but to kill them. Their killer instincts didn't extend to the chickens or sheep, which were treated as their charges, to be protected.

Chapter

16

New Additions

$Since\ we$ didn't have day-to-day communications of events outside of Akutan, and often not outside our own little world at the head of the bay, we couldn't monitor the status of the Land Freeze, so continued our daily lives as if there would be no consequences. Charlie and I had strengthened our relationship and enjoyed working as a couple. We were finally experiencing the life we'd envisioned back in the early '60s when we first talked of starting a ranch on an isolated island. That now seemed so long ago.

While we went about our daily chores, all of us kept a close eye on the two very pregnant sows, already large animals when we got them and still growing into immense creatures. One day, as Slick and Fish Head roamed and rooted about the land near our cabin, I observed a peculiar sight. Both of them hauled small bunches of tall dry yellow grass using their snouts, and piled their little bundles in separate mounds. This activity progressed till the mounds looked like small rectangular hay stacks. I had never raised pigs so I was also surprised by what followed.

On a rare sunny morning in June as I walked out back behind the cabin, the stacks looked much bigger than the day before. I approached out of curiosity and noted a large pig snout sticking out of each mound. Maybe it was some sort of animal instinct that caused them to make their own outdoor shelters, using what was available to them. They managed to get the stacks the proper size, then crawled in and covered themselves so well a stranger would probably think we had just piled big stacks of hay for feed. Those pigs must not have been familiar with what happened to the first little pig in the fairytale, *The Three Little Pigs*. But then there were no wolves on Akutan, and the dogs kept the foxes at bay.

That same day I advised the children to stay away from the mounds. "I don't know what's going on, but I think it best not to disturb Slick Pig and Fish Head, and you two keep your little brother away from them when you're outside."

One morning the big sows didn't leave their man-made shelter to head for their daytime pig-made shelter. Since this was a break in their routine, Charlie and Hans entered their pen to check on them and found them lying on their sides, soundlessly expelling little creatures, no more than eight or nine inches long. The piglets were a variety of shades and colors from all pinkish-white to completely black or tan, or a blend of two of the colors. Leaving Hans there, Charlie ran back to the cabin to tell us what was happening, then returned to the scene, keeping the gate closed. When Becky and Malcolm ran over to see what was happening, trailed by Eric, Charlie called to them. "You kids stay out of the pen, keep an eye on your little brother and don't make noise."

They did the next best thing as they climbed on the pen rails and leaned far over in order to see what they could. Every so often inside the shelter, they heard Hans say, "Dere comes anoter one!" He could well have said it several dozen times.

I watched for a little while but there were so many of them and it was taking a long time. I had my usual daily chores to attend to, and with all the others at the pig pen I was able to get more done.

By nightfall there was a mass of squirming, wriggling little bodies all over the floor of that shed. The multiple deliveries produced twelve in one litter and thirteen in the other. When we went out to check on them early the next morning, we approached cautiously. The now not-quite-so-huge sows still lay on their sides as the little babies had their first breakfast on

Our cabin, completed in December, 1967, was located near the beach and about three-fourths of a mile from the hills surrounding it.

A small group of Hereford cattle are in front of our cabin, which is close to the beach. A few pigs often followed them around.

Summer of '68. I am holding one of the twenty-five piglets, all born on the same day.

Akutan. They rudely pushed, shoved and climbed over each other trying to get at a teat, some crowded out by the more aggressive. Fortunately, pigs can have as many as twelve teats, so they are prepared for large numbers at one time, though with twenty-five piglets between them there would always be some scrambling. We tried not to get too close to the scene or make any sudden moves and disturb them. Though Slick and Fish Head lay quite still, they tracked us suspiciously with their bright dark eyes, as if ready to spring if we made any sudden moves. They had generally been fairly relaxed around us prior to motherhood, especially Slick.

Later that day the mothers left the pen as the gate was left open for them. They headed for their haystack shelters, followed by twenty-five miniature creatures that looked very much like children's colorful little stuffed dolls with their mixed shades of pinks, browns and blacks. Though they moved as fast as they could the newborns lagged behind as they trotted on tiny stumps of legs. The tired sows didn't look back and didn't slow down, as if they were deliberately trying to get away from the hoard of little parasites for a while. When they reached the mounds they burrowed right in and arranged themselves on their sides. Not too long after, the progeny reached their respective mothers, though I don't know if they really made a distinction. After approaching the resting sows, they immediately began their nursing ritual of pushing, shoving and vying for position.

As the days went by, the piglets grew rather rapidly and seemed to be all over the area around the cabin. They were still in their cute stage and made great pets for the children.

One day when it began raining heavily, Fish Head lumbered inside the chicken house instead of the pig shed and settled down, trailed by a few of

Hans, Eric and one of our many pet pigs, which were later traded to fishing boats for fuel and food staples.

her litter. In the meantime, the range chickens began heading for their shelter, but after they stuck their heads inside the open door and saw the unfriendly Fish Head in their house they congregated in clusters outside in the rain. We were all outside trying to help animals get to shelter from the rainstorm when Charlie saw the clumps of drenched chickens huddled outside their own doorway.

He yelled, "What's wrong with those dumb chickens, don't they have enough sense to get in out of the rain?"

By now the rain was coming down sideways, pushed by strong winds. When he approached them to shoo them in, with Malcolm by his side, he saw their problem. Suddenly, it was Malcolm's problem. Charlie had other situations to deal with.

"Get that pig outta there," he ordered his son, who would have to go in and drive a creature at least five or six times his weight, out into the storm. It was like David and Goliath. But would the modern-day David win? Malcolm didn't really want to do it. None of us liked to be around Fish Head because of her generally unfriendly disposition. But I never heard Malcolm talk back to his father or argue with him. I know it was not out of any parental fear, but out of respect; he knew his father to be an easy-going man, and on the rare occasion that he gave a direct order there must be a good reason.

Malcolm got a big stick for protection and went in. Fish Head wasn't used to taking orders from anybody. After staring Malcolm down, which didn't work, she raised her huge body, stood on all fours, glared at him with black beady eyes, and acted like she was headed for the door. Suddenly, she turned her head, lunged at him and bit him hard on the inner thigh. Malcolm let out a yell. A lesser David would have run from his oversized opponent, but Malcolm stood his ground. He poked her a few times with the stick, as he stayed behind her. She moved reluctantly toward the doorway, then went out into the rainstorm, followed by several piglets. Some very wet hens with plastered down feathers scurried into their dry home. Fish Head took off for her own shelter, leaving behind an injured but triumphant eight year old victor. Later, Malcolm showed us the large bruise and broken skin on his leg and said he had been petrified with fear at the time but he was going to get her out of there. While the biblical David fought for a king, our modern-day warrior fought for some helpless and frightened wet chickens.

Both pigs seemed to tire of motherhood rather quickly, maybe because they found out what all it entailed. They tried to get away from those cute little piglets at every opportunity. Slick became our friend again, and occasionally Fish Head, who even allowed us to approach her, though I always treated her with caution, trying to detect her mood before getting close. Sometimes they came up to the cabin door that we usually left open if it was not too cold or stormy, as it provided more light. When they did that I gave them scraps, which I felt encouraged them to stay in the area and to trust me.

Slick spent a lot of time following Becky and Malcolm around whenever they were outside. She seemed to prefer their company to her own progeny. But they didn't always welcome hers, especially when they played hide and seek. Of course the game was just supposed to involve Becky and Malcolm, but Slick did not disqualify herself. She would follow the one who was hiding and, with her monstrous pink rear end sticking out, give away the hiding place, despite all efforts to shoo her away. They enjoyed her company but at times she could be a nuisance.

Since the pigs seemed to do well on the island—we now had twenty-seven—we purchased two wiener pigs, the kind you see at pig roasts, from the Choates at Unalaska that summer. The two new additions were already a few months old, and were just for fattening as it would take quite a while for our own litters to be ready to be sold. We kept the new ones in the pen most of the time and gave them lots of food. They seemed content just to do their job, eat and get fat.

In time we had lots of pork to eat and occasionally mutton, plus eggs and chickens. We traded eggs and small pigs ready for butchering, with the fishing boats that occasionally came up to the head of the bay. We didn't have much money so the barter system worked well for us. They, in turn, provided us with fresh produce such as apples and oranges, besides barrels of oil for our stove.

In the midst of our contentment we received another addition to our growing head of the bay population—this time of a human variety.

Chapter

17

Surprise Visitor

$On\ a$ sunny day that July of '68 we took the dory to the village to visit with friends. Though it was 'plane day', that wasn't what brought us to town; it was the calm weather. The excitement of the arrival of the mail plane had worn off some time ago, unless we were expecting something, which we were not. It was the one time we really should have gone down to meet the Goose.

Late that afternoon, the six of us headed home in the dory, and as we drew near the beach we saw someone sitting there on something. No skiff was around, so we wondered who it could be. Perhaps someone had walked from the village, which people did occasionally, and finding us gone decided to await our return in order to visit.

Soon we could make out the person sitting there, a black-haired woman wearing glasses. As she waved at us, Charlie shouted over the noise of the engine, "It's Opal!" She was Charlie's older sister, about fifty. We all waved back and beached the boat, then headed toward her. She raised from her suitcase chair, looking much like I'd remembered her, slender, medium height.

"Opal, what the hell are you doing here? How'd you get here?" he called to her, smiling broadly.

"Hi, Buck." She called him by his childhood nickname, short for Buckwheat. Then she hugged her brother and said hi to the rest of us. She looked at Hans and asked, "Who is that?"

"My partner, Hans Radtke."

"Hello, Hans Radtke," she said in her open friendly way, a lot like Charlie.

"Hello to you," he responded.

"Let's get inside, then you can tell us what's going on," Charlie said. We hadn't seen her since the spring of '60, over eight years ago, when we visited his mother in New Mexico. Once inside, Opal told us, "I got on a plane in New Mexico, then after four planes and many hours I landed at Akutan. You really are isolated."

She did all of this without communicating with us. We hadn't been in touch with her since the spring of '65, over three years ago, just before sailing for Akutan, when Charlie called her.

Opal continued, "When I arrived here I didn't know where you lived. I asked an older man who was on the beach when I got off the plane and he pointed in this direction and said that's where your cabin was. When I asked how I could get there, he graciously offered to take me here in his skiff. Then when we got here he said your dory wasn't on the beach. He didn't know where you were but figured you'd be back soon, since you could never be gone too long with all the livestock around your cabin. There were chickens and pigs running around all over the place. I told him I'd just wait on the beach till you showed up. It hasn't been very long."

Charlie asked, "Why didn't you let us know you were coming?"

"It was a spur of the moment decision. I retired as a school nurse and Fred retired about the same time, but to the golf course. I got tired of being a golf widow and decided to do something adventurous, like go see my baby brother in Alaska. I didn't figure he'd notice I was gone for a day or two." I remembered she always had a funny way of putting things. But that was a pretty gutsy story. She was fifty years old and had never been to Alaska.

Charlie asked, "Well, have you notified Fred yet?"

"At the airport between my first and second plane, I called him. I was already on my way and had my ticket clear to Akutan, so there was no turning back."

While Charlie, the youngest of ten children, was the fifth of six sons to venture to Alaska, Opal was the first of the four daughters to make that trip.

Our accommodations were still pretty limited and primitive, though we now had cold water running to the house from a hillside waterfall. Having been raised in similar conditions on her parents' ranch back in the '20s and '30s, Opal reverted to her roots as she fixed up a corner of the cabin for herself. She wasn't a fussy person so she fit right in. The atmosphere in that one main room began to feel slightly cramped, yet homey as our family grew to seven, in a space of about 16x20 feet. The remaining bit of space was still partitioned off for storage. As I look back, I don't remember feeling crowded, but then we didn't have much, either. It was sort of like camping on a long term basis.

A few days after Opal's arrival, a large king crab processor came into the bay and tied up at the rotting abandoned dock at the old whaling station, the only time I ever saw a boat tie up there. The dock was full of holes large enough to step through, so we always looked down when we walked on it. It rested on rotting, broken pilings that no longer supported one end of the dock, which sagged noticeably. Shortly after the boat docked we observed several men walking the quarter mile from the processor toward our place.

When we went out to meet them, one man asked, "Is Joan Brown here? I heard she's done relief cooking on boats occasionally."

"I'm Joan. Come on in. Yes, I've cooked on a few processors over in Dutch Harbor when a cook would take a short vacation."

As he entered the cluttered cabin, he said, "Our cook is flying out to-morrow for a couple weeks' vacation and return on the following flight. We're really in a bind as we haven't been able to find a replacement and then someone told us about you. So here we are."

This was a surprise. I didn't know where he'd heard about me, perhaps from one of the processors I'd cooked for. It's a small world, to be offered a job in such a far flung place and when you least expect it. I already had plenty to do with my usual chores, plus the new pigs, and Opal's arrival, so I was just listening politely, but wasn't particularly interested.

He continued, "I know this is short notice, and I realize it might be a challenge to cook three meals a day for about ninety men." That was the first mention of the number of people on board, though the size of the processor, which looked big enough to be an ex- landing craft, should have been a clue. I tried to restrain my startled expression, but was apparently unsuccessful.

Before I balked, he quickly added, "You'd have a cook's helper." Then he offered me a very good salary. I forgot about my chores, the pigs, Opal. I had done quantity cooking on a few occasions, and had prepared food for some fairly large groups, maybe up to sixty, but this would be a record breaker.

Even before I responded, Opal chimed in. "I'll help you and I don't want to be paid. I like to cook."

"Okay, I'll take the job and I'll bring Opal with me. I know there'll be a lot of work and long hours and I could use the extra help." I could see the man's demeanor relax.

They headed out the cabin door with Opal and me and we walked to the processor. Once aboard, they introduced us to the cook, so he could show Opal and me around.

Then the cook introduced us to his helper. His duties were to bring in the daily supplies for me, a job for a strong person, as large cans of vegetables and burlap bags of dry goods had to be hauled to the galley from the store room first thing every day. In order to prepare two hundred seventy meals a day, a lot of supplies had to be brought in. He would also assist with the food preparations. After meeting him and being told all this, it didn't really seem overwhelming. I did wonder if he had some misgivings about me, though, as I barely weighed a hundred pounds and quantity cooking some-times requires real muscle. But I knew I could manage. I wasn't a city girl anymore. Working with farm animals kept me in pretty good shape.

Besides the crew, eighty men worked on the processor, mostly Eskimo, including the foreman. King crab was plentiful in those days and there weren't all the conservation restrictions that came later, so the boat was a pretty busy place.

Back in college I took a class in quantity cooking for up to seventy-five people as part of a home economics minor. I had to take it for an entire semester and wondered why such an unnecessary class was a requirement to complete the minor. Ten years later, on a remote island, my question was answered.

From our front yard, the village is to the left about two miles away. On the right the old Whaling Station is about a quarter mile from us. A processor is temporarily tied to the rotting dock, and on the hillside above the dock huge storage tanks from the old whaling days can be seen.

Opal and I returned to the cabin and I told Charlie about my new job. "I've accepted the cooking job and Opal's going to help me," I said with enthusiasm.

I expected him to be glad that we'd have a little more money coming in, so I was surprised at his response.

"Who's going to watch the kids? How long is this job?"

"It's for two weeks, just between planes." I avoided the question about the kids.

"You know the plane is sometimes delayed up to a week. Does that mean you might work as long as three weeks?" He was still being negative.

"Well, the good part is I'd make another week's pay."

"So how are you going to care for the three kids? Who's going to fix our meals? Hans and I are pretty busy right now."

I started to get annoyed. "You can take charge of the kids during the day. Malcolm can help you and Hans, and Becky can handle the meals. She already does a lot of the cooking and baking, anyway. She's almost twelve; she's been cooking since she was eight years old. I don't have to do every-thing around here. She can help keep an eye on Eric. She already does that, too. It'll work out, you'll see." I sensed an argument coming on; I was glad his sister was there and she was on my side.

Opal chimed in. "Stop being unreasonable. We'll be right back after we serve the evening meal and Joan and I can take care of the kids then, or whatever else there is to do. I want to do this, Buck." She called him by his childhood nickname. Now I knew he would relent. Of his other eight siblings, Opal was probably closest to him since she was twelve when he was born and had assumed the duty of second mother as he was growing up.

So I wasn't surprised when he said, "Yeah, I guess you're right." End of discussion.

The next day I began my new career as 'Supercook.' I felt a little nervous about it so I was glad to have Opal along. We walked the quarter mile to my new job. As we walked across the rotting dock, we made sure to keep our eyes down to avoid stepping through the holes.

When we got there, various helpful notes were on the counter, along with a menu outline to follow. The evening dessert on the menu for that first day was lemon meringue pie. The pies would have to be made from scratch, no prepared pie crusts and no packages of lemon filling or bottled lemon juice. It seemed a little presumptuous of the cook to put that on my first day's menu. What was wrong with Jello or canned peaches? Had the men been asking for pie and he didn't want to do it? I didn't know, but I took it in stride. The men were in for a treat as others had told me that my crusts were especially good, a skill I passed on to my daughter when she was only nine. After my other cooking chores were completed, I proceeded to make fifteen pie crusts that first afternoon, the most I'd ever prepared at one time. While I made the dough, Opal made the from-scratch lemon filling that required her to squeeze a whole bunch of fresh lemons; last came the meringue. Our reward was the thanks we received from many of the ninety men. I felt we got off to a good start with the guys and was comfortable about any screw-ups that might happen later, though conveniently I don't remember there ever having been any.

We used a large galvanized metal garbage can for all our food prep scraps, like vegetable peelings and scrapings from the workers' plates. One of the best perks of the job was that the boss told me I could take the can home every evening and feed the scraps to the many pigs of various sizes that we'd accumulated. When the cook returned a few weeks later—the only time I wouldn't have minded a plane delay—the processor pulled out. I think the pigs missed the boat as much as I missed a paying job and doing work I enjoyed.

While Opal and I worked on the processor, Hans took off for crab fishing as a deck hand out of Dutch Harbor. Charlie took care of the ranch with the help of Becky and Malcolm till the cooking job ended. Then he could spend more time with Opal, and I got back to my cabin chores, which included taking care of Eric who, at almost two, was well into the inquisitive stage, plus the toddler rebellion stage, not unlike teenage rebellion. Everyone kept an eye on him though it was no one's assigned duty. Becky and Malcolm usually had their own plans, which mostly involved the outdoors, so Eric was safer indoors where he was easier to watch, but even then nothing could suppress his curious nature.

Summer of '68, my little cowboy, Eric, age 2, who didn't like to wear shoes.

He explored everything he could within his reach, plus the more challenging attractions that required climbing skills, at which he became quite adept.

I ordered Eric hard soled white leather training shoes from Sears now that he was walking, but he did not appreciate the expense I went to, even though money was tight. No sooner did I put them on him, laced and tied, then he would clomp off to the dark storage part of the cabin, and shortly thereafter reappear barefoot and happy. I retrieved the detested shoes from behind the partition each time and went through the motions again, only to see him emerge triumphantly into the light a short time later, shoeless and trying not to catch my eye. Opal came to my rescue, though she did not endear herself to her little nephew. After one of his expeditions into the dark, Opal was waiting for him. She retrieved the abandoned shoes.

"Come here, Eric. Let me show you a little trick," she said with a smile.

When he hesitantly approached her, she sat him in her lap, pulled on his shoes, and tied the bows in double knots. When he slid off her lap she turned her back so he'd have an opportunity to hide and begin the process at which he thought he excelled. After a longer time than usual, accompanied by some muffled thumping, he emerged with a pouty look. He couldn't say anything because he was supposed to wear those hated shoes. Opal and I made no comment, as we ignored him, pretending not to notice that he appeared a little upset. After that, she took over the job of shoeing him every morning.

After Hans returned from fishing that summer, Charlie left shortly afterward in August, on the F/V *Rosemary*, a crab boat run by Del Valley out of Kodiak. Opal was still with us, and during that time her twenty-fifth wedding anniversary occurred. Even though her husband, Fred, wouldn't be there, we decided to have a little celebration since it was a special occasion. We dug out our dress-up clothes and shook out some of the wrinkles. Hans put on his only suit and a button-front shirt and I had sport jackets for Malcolm and Eric, though the sleeves were a little short by then. Opal, Becky and I wore dresses, a rarity since work clothes were the usual order of the day. Becky and I hadn't worn dresses since we left Anchorage as they were not suited to our present lifestyle.

I made a special cake, a single layer, with white icing and wrote Happy 25th Wedding Anniversary on it. Then I made an icing design of a stick-man with a golf club and a stick woman on an island (it had a little palm tree—not politically correct). Those decorations were rather primitive; my artistic ability was limited to working with oils. Opal seemed very happy that we had made such a festive occasion of her anniversary and all of us enjoyed her party. There was rarely an opportunity to dress up for anything at the cabin, but I wanted to do something memorable for my sister-in-law on her special day.

Opal applied for work in the hospital at Nome. She received notice of

Late summer, 1968. Becky is holding one of the piglets, with Sugar, our very smart Australian Shepard, standing by. The barn, our first home, is in the background. The old abandoned Whaling Station can be seen in the distance. The crab processor tied up to its rotting dock is where I cooked for a crew of 90 for a few weeks.

her acceptance the end of August, so she took off on the next plane. Eric would surely miss her. Actually, they seemed to bond, though she always corrected his behavior by prefacing it with, "Let me show you a little trick."

By fall of '68 I decided to take the children to Anchorage again for the next school year, as the home schooling hadn't worked out as I'd planned, with classes running well into June. I used my two weeks' salary from the processor to finance the trip, so we left shortly after Opal. Hans agreed to spend the winter taking care of the animals while Charlie fished on the *Rosemary*. We would need more funds if we were to restock, despite the Land Claims issue. We had regressed to small farm status with the huge stock losses and were destined to remain there unless we could come up with a plan to turn things around. Though remote, the possibility was still there that we would get the home site so we didn't want to give up on the ranch, not yet.

The cows did well on Akutan and were less trouble than the sheep, so we wanted to increase the herd and drop the sheep if we could come up with the money. Charlie and I planned to save enough money working that winter of '68-'69, while Hans watched the ranch. The whole operation and surrounding events had used up our initial funds, but we had too much invested to give up if there was any way we could hang on, at least till Congress made a decision.

Unfortunately, there wasn't an opening at the employment office so I worked as an RN at the local hospital, but the salary was far less than the previous job. Charlie made very little money crab fishing so on Christmas Eve he got off the *Rosemary* in Kodiak and flew to Anchorage to look for work. Since I was barely getting by with what I made, living paycheck to paycheck I too hadn't been able to save any money. It was a much different situation financially from when we were in Anchorage a few years before. By the time Charlie found work in February we knew there wouldn't be any money for restocking.

We applied for a bank loan, though our original loan still had two more annual spring payments remaining. Naturally, the bank officer wanted us to list what the money would be for and what it would cost. So we contacted a farm in Palmer, about forty miles from Anchorage, and were told they'd have some calves to sell in the spring. We checked on a barge out of Homer, about two hundred miles from Anchorage, but it was quite large and was very expensive so that wouldn't work.

Then I called Reeve Aleutian Airways to see if they could haul calves in a cargo plane to Unalaska and we could find a way to get them to Akutan. The owner, Bob Reeve, who founded the airline a year before I was born, answered the phone himself, much to my surprise. He said it was feasible though it would be expensive. In the middle of our phone conversation, he said, "I've gotta' hang up. My tomato soup is burning." He was a very informal person.

With all this information we returned to the bank to pursue our loan. We didn't have much experience with that process, and quickly learned that banks don't just loan money because people ask. By spring we were

Becky, Malcolm and Eric are standing on the deck in front of our cabin, August, 1968. Fencing for the surviving sheep from Akun is in the background. In 2001, when Doug went to the head of the bay, he saw some of the fence posts still standing.

notified that we were turned down. Apparently, our operation didn't look all that promising to the bank. When we contacted BLM, they agreed to reduce the stock requirements as they were aware of our animal losses, but we still had the same lease payment as it was based on the amount of land. Charlie used his salary he'd made that spring working for an oil company, to pay the annual lease fee and the agricultural loan payment, but it took almost all of his earnings. Both institutions wanted real money, not eggs or pigs.

Charlie left us in Anchorage and headed back to Akutan to help Hans that spring of '69, and then to take over the ranch work so Hans could head for salmon fishing as a deckhand in Bristol Bay. Charlie would also have to give Hans the bad news about restocking. Maybe Hans would have a good fishing season and we could reconsider our plan.

Chapter

18

Living off the Land

When school ended that May of '69, the children and I were anxious to return to Akutan to rejoin Charlie. Though the ranch situation was no better, we preferred the Aleutians to city living. We took a few small animals back with us.

After we picked up a few things for the ranch at a feed store we saw some fuzzy yellow ducklings for sale there and ended up with four. They were so tiny one could fit into the palm of my hand, so I put them into a very small carton. The store also had some funny looking creatures, barely as big as the ducklings, with black and white feathers. The clerk told us they were African guinea hens that lived in the wild in their native land and full grown would not be much bigger than a pigeon. Somehow, these had found their way into to an Anchorage feed store. Two of them were going to find their way to Akutan. I purchased them for their unique appearance, but they turned out to be rather unusual in other ways, too.

Fortunately there weren't security checks at the airport in those days. The ducks went as a carryon in a small cardboard box, unsealed except for the closed flaps. Becky carried the ducklings while Malcolm carried a carton with the two little hens. We were able to board the plane without problems as the animals were silent. Once on the plane it was a different matter. Becky had to keep pushing one yellow duck head after the other back inside the box opening, which got them aroused enough to start quacking, not peeping—they were a few weeks old by then. The stewardess didn't seem to notice, though, over the roar of the DC6. Fortunately the two small guinea hens were silent; they were good travelers. We transferred to the Goose and made it to Akutan without any problems. I felt the ducklings should enjoy their new home with its limitless availability of water, but it remained to be seen how the little hens would be able to adapt to their new home far from the Kalahari Dessert.

Once we reached Akutan after the long flight from Anchorage, we placed the six new additions in the chicken house with the remaining hens and few roosters. From their first morning the four ducks headed single file for the nearby creek, followed single file by two little black and white striped African guinea hens. The ducks spent their days sitting in the shallow icy water; the two small creatures at first followed them into the creek and attempted to swim. They discovered that didn't work and quickly retreated to the bank, squatting in the grass till evening when they returned to their shelter waddling single file at the end of the line behind the ducks. Inside the chicken house, the hens and roosters slept on roosts, normal chicken fashion. The ducks slept on the floor, normal duck fashion, alongside two little guinea hens that thought they were ducks.

The children and I resettled into the cabin after our ten month hiatus and life continued very much as before. Becky and Malcolm were used to the isolation and freedom of remote places so there was no adjustment period or regret at leaving the big city, even with all its advantages.

Sugar and Malt showed their joy for the return of the children by following them everywhere, often racing with them up and down the beach. I usually kept Eric in the cabin with me while I did the indoor chores, so he wouldn't wander down to the water, and he kept himself busy getting into whatever he could reach.

Hans would not return from fishing till late July, so Becky, now twelve, and Malcolm, nine, helped Charlie with the animal chores. Both children helped with Eric when I let him go outside.

Besides our usual tasks, we butchered and cleaned the few remaining chickens and sold them to the fishing boats and the local people, along with pork, mutton, and fresh eggs till the hens were gone. With almost no money, we bartered for items such as stove oil, gasoline, flour, and sugar. We counted heavily on Hans having a good salmon season as money was needed to maintain what little was left of the ranch while awaiting word on the Land Claims settlement.

We had not yet given up hope for the federal home site grant, which required that we continue to occupy the property even if the original ranch failed, but without additional funds living there was becoming increasingly difficult. We wanted Akutan to be our home. All of us liked the lifestyle and proximity to the friendly unsophisticated village. While it was the sixties, I don't think we thought of ourselves as part of the counterculture. We weren't your stereotypical hippies that were flooding the nation, driven by drugs, music or anti-war sentiments, but something inside all of us seemed to want a simpler life. Even 'the simple life' requires some money, so we looked forward with great expectation to Hans' return.

Salmon runs go in cycles and that year the run was poor, though I was not that familiar with salmon habits at the time. Some boats did fair, but for Hans it was a disastrous season. He returned with a very small paycheck for all his efforts. In previous years he described the nets as so full it took a great deal of effort to pull them in. This time it was not uncommon for the net to contain no more than seven or eight fish each time. It was a discouraging run but normal in the overall scheme of things. He was as downhearted as we were when he had to tell us.

After the three children jumped all over their Uncle Hansie when he came in the door and gave them big hugs, Charlie said, "You kids go outside now and play for a bit. I got to talk some business with Hans."

After they climbed out of Hans' lap and ran out the makeshift door, I yelled, "Watch your little brother," though I didn't need to say it as Becky and Malcolm took that responsibility seriously.

Charlie looked at Hans and me and said solemnly, "Time for a family conference." We had hoped to avoid this discussion as long as possible, but we had to face reality. Too many things had gone wrong.

"If one of us can get hired on a boat this winter, maybe we could last till spring. I hate giving all this up and none of us really wants to leave, it's just we gotta have money for fuel and food this winter. And in the spring we still have the lease payment and the final agriculture loan payment." He was just verbalizing everything we already knew.

"Vell, I have a little bit of money from fishing so maybe it can hold us for a while till something comes along," Hans said. "In the meantime, I think ve should start selling everyting ve can. This ranch is never going to support us. And getting a home site is not going to happen, regardless of how the Land Claims is settled."

"You don't know that!" My voice got louder. "Are you saying just give up the ranch? You're just being negative, Hans. The children and I came back here because we want to live here. I know things are bad but maybe they'll get better." I didn't like the reality thrust on me so bluntly, though I knew that was just his way. I just didn't want to hear it then. I was happier here than any place I'd ever lived. All of us loved the life, so it was depressing to even talk about our venture coming to such an abrupt end.

"Get real, Joan," he said sharply. "I'm just being practical. I vant to stay here, too, but ve have to make a living. Maybe you don't mind living like this, but dere's tree kids to support. Ve got to find a way to take care of dem."

Charlie usually took over the role of pacifier, so he tried to calm me down and also soften some of Hans' stark assessments. "Okay, let's wait a while. We don't have any money to leave with, anyway, and no place to go. Hans just got back. Let's talk about this later. We'll start selling off stock since there's no way we'll ever again build up the count to BLM requirements. There's those cows over in Hot Springs Bay, but no incentive in the world's ever gonna get 'em back over the mountain to this side. They've found a nice warm home with year 'round grazing so they don't need us. They've proved they can survive without us."

Not all of the various turns of events over the past four years had been bad. I was in favor of hanging on, but agreed with selling off everything we could. Our stay there could come to an end even before we would find out whether we were going to get our home site, but in the meantime we would carry on as we had been.

A plume from Akutan Volcano can be seen when facing the bay in the late '60's when there was some activity that lasted for a while. We could smell the stink of sulfur in the air sometimes, and often soot showed up on our faces.

One morning late that summer, a skiff pulled up on our beach. Four people, including a small child, climbed out and headed toward our cabin. We recognized Peter, but the other three people were strangers to us, or so we thought. Charlie, with the rest of us following, went out to meet them and as they approached, Charlie had instant recognition.

"Max Meeker!" he said loudly, in surprise.

"Hi, Brownie," the tall slender young man replied, after a short pause, probably just as startled.

They had not seen each other for ten or eleven years, certainly not since Charlie graduated from Western New Mexico University in Silver City back in '58. They didn't even run in the same circles, plus Max was a year or two ahead of Charlie, working on his Master's. I hadn't known Max so I didn't know who he was, but they each knew who the other was, so maybe they hadn't changed that much over the years. Max introduced the young slim woman with him as his wife, Sue. The little blonde preschooler was their daughter, Hanna Sue.

They arrived in Akutan a few days before, when someone in the village mentioned the name of the rancher (at least, someone still referred to him as that) at the head of the bay and that he was originally from New Mexico. Max had no idea that Charlie Brown was the person whom he had known as Brownie, since Charlie never used his given name of Charles till he came to Alaska to teach back in '58. Back then, some of the teachers had started calling him Chuck, which he disliked just as much, so he said to call him Charlie and it stuck—even with me. I had called him Brownie till we were in Seward.

Max was just curious to meet a person who was from his home state—one of life's many coincidences.

Once we were all settled into the cabin, Max explained that he was hired to teach at Akutan Elementary for the coming year. Of all the elementary schools in all the fifty states, Max picked the one that was six or seven thousand miles from his hometown, only to discover that one of the members of the only other non-Aleut family living there had played football against him in high school in New Mexico, and had attended the same small teacher's college at about the same time. It was 'old home week' as they caught up on what they had been doing over the years.

After that initial visit, I was really impressed with Max and wanted Becky and Malcolm to attend the Akutan School and have him for a teacher, but we were so broke we couldn't even afford to rent Uncle Paul's cabin. I planned to homeschool them yet again, though I would have liked for Becky to spend her last year in grade school in a real classroom and have the memory of a formal graduation. She had always been a good student though and an avid reader, with her nose in a thick book every chance she got, so I knew she would do just fine. I had already sent my order off to Juneau in plenty of time so that their materials should arrive before the start of the school year this time.

19

Struggling to Survive

By August, we still traded and sold eggs and animals in exchange for oil and food supplies as we no longer had money available for those purchases. I didn't know how we would get through the winter, but the guys still thought they might get deckhand jobs. Hans often did well and was popular with skippers, but Charlie was like an albatross on boats, dooming them to financial disaster. Do albatrosses affect ranches, too?

As our food supply continued to dwindle, the local people seemed aware of our struggles, probably because we went there fairly often to sell other things besides animal products. One day I asked Anesia Kudrin if I could hold a 'garage sale' in Uncle Paul's cabin since it was just sitting there empty. Always gracious, she didn't want money for it so I had Charlie bring me to town for my one day sale. I was able to sell a few of my paintings. Martha Mensoff, my former fifth grader Jimmy's mother, bought an oil painting of a toddler sitting on a potty with reams of toilet paper all around him. Someone else bought a large seascape pastel and gave it to Reeve Aleutian Airways for their Anchorage office, though I never found out what they really did with that donation. A few of the women bought some of my clothes, the dressier stuff that hadn't seen much wear—totally unsuited to feeding chickens—plus other surplus things such as LP records, that I couldn't play anyway. I didn't need those things but I did need other things for the children, mainly food.

Finally we ran out of chicken feed. Without money to purchase more feed or any other kind of feed, including human feed for that matter, we ate or sold the remaining chickens.

With no more fresh eggs, Peter Stepetin brought us some seagull eggs. I had never tried them. "Ignaty and I went out in the skiff and got a bunch for anyone in the village that wanted some. I figured you might be able to use some now that you don't have chickens."

I thought how we had sold and traded our chicken eggs in the village and Peter was just sharing his and Ignaty's supply with us, asking nothing in return. At first, the idea of eating any kind of eggs but chicken or duck seemed too foreign to me, like eating raw sea urchins which my children tried with other kids in town. But I realized how insulting it would be to turn down the gesture, plus his ancestors had managed to survive for centuries by living off the land, and I was in survival mode.

"Thank you, Peter. How do you fix them?"

"One of my favorites is spice cake made with them, but fix them however you want."

Later, when I would make a cake, for instance, none of us could tell any difference; maybe we were just too hungry to notice. I felt like I'd just passed my first test in Survival School.

Blueberries and moss berries were plentiful in the marshy land near our farm compound, so we picked lots on the days it wasn't too windy or stormy. People from the village came there to gather some, also, and stopped in to see us. Because of our isolation, I was lonely sometimes for the company of others so it was a treat when they showed up and I could have them in for a cup of tea. We always drank tea out of mugs, but one time a fishing boat came up to the head of the bay and a skiff went ashore; they often did to trade books. The skipper was middle-aged and attired more like a gentleman fisherman than a working one, definitely not dressed like the crew member he brought with him. When I served him tea in a mug, he informed me that I should have given him a saucer for his mug. It was said in a superior

As 1969 approached, the pigpen with its shelter on the far right was now vacant, as was the chicken house, attached to the back of the barn on the right. But we hadn't given up.

manner, as if talking to the help. There went my tip. Though I did comply with his request, I never saw him again. Maybe he thought I would forget again. Thank goodness he didn't ask for sugar.

Bright red spawning salmon appeared in our creek at an opportune time for us—or so I thought. "Becky, why don't you and Malcolm go sharpen some long sticks and see if you can get a couple of those salmon and we could have some for dinner."

They thought that sounded like something fun to do, so they took off in search of long sticks. With no trees there they went to the lumber scrap pile. In about an hour they had each speared one of those bright red fish and called their dad to clean them. Then they ran up to the house to tell me about their successful fishing venture.

"It was so easy, Mom. That was fun," Malcolm said with a grin.

"Well, I don't want you doing it unless I tell you. We're just doing it because we're a little low on food, right now."

I turned up the stove to boil the water, though we were now limiting the amount of oil we burned, trying to make it last till something 'broke' for us. When Charlie brought the cleaned fish in I cut it up and put it in the hot water. Later, I called everyone in to get a plate and eat.

They helped themselves to some of the fish and I fixed a little plate for Eric. The others had already started, sitting on their double duty bed/sofas when Malcolm said," I don't like it," and took it out of his mouth.

Then Charlie piped in, "You don't have to eat it. This is awful."

Hans said, "I thought I could eat anyting!" as he pushed his plate away.

Eric was already spitting fish out when I took my first bite.

"This tastes like mud!" I exclaimed. At least, it was my idea of what mud tasted like.

Charlie took his plate out on the deck where Sugar and Malt were sitting. They gobbled it up. But then their palates had not been spoiled by commercial dog food. Plus, they were getting few, if any, table scraps, now that they had to compete with us. I was glad to have found a source of food for them for a little while—and the kids seemed to enjoy their new chore of getting an occasional fish for the dogs.

Besides bringing us the bird eggs, periodically a couple of men from the village went out in a skiff and killed a sea lion and shared the meat with other families. Luke, the former village chief, often brought us some of the liver, as it was extremely large, so there was plenty to go around. My children didn't like liver of any kind, no matter what animal it came from nor how hungry they were. They had probably put it in a category with bright red salmon. But Charlie, Hans and I liked it very much, and were glad to get it. When it came to living off the land, we were quick learners. Being almost out of food and money is a great motivator.

We even tried the small octopus that could be flushed from the large, partially submerged rocks along the beach toward the village. I'd never cooked it before, so when I did it came out like rubber. Only Charlie and Hans ate it. They were either hungrier or had better teeth. I learned later that you don't boil octopus, but I didn't have a recipe for preparing it in my old *Better Homes and Gardens* cookbook.

That September we lost our sheep dog, Malt, the yellow haired one. She had been with us from that first summer. She was lying stretched out on the deck in front of the cabin one morning with a trickle of blood along the side of her mouth. We never knew for sure what happened. It was almost like a death in the family, as we were so used to her being with us all the time through all our adventures and misadventures. We had taken her presence for granted so it was hard for us to get used to seeing Sugar all alone, since the two had been inseparable all those years, doing everything together. They worked as a well- choreographed team, Malt always following Sugar in her nonverbal commands, an obedient yet intelligent dog.

After that, Sugar became more and more of a house dog now that she was alone, and with her apparent understanding of our language it was sort of like having another person in the room. She seldom barked or made much noise, just looked at us with her soulful eyes and sad expression, which sort of gave her a knowing look.

Early in September when the Goose was due, the bay was calm enough to land and bring the mail, so Hans took the dory to town the next day to check if the boxes from Juneau with the school supplies came in. Not surprisingly, the weather had changed that morning and the wind had picked up, making the bay rough. Hans had a bouncy two-mile trip back and when he pulled up on our beach amidst some breaking waves, a lot of water came over the side of the boat. We ran out to help him as he climbed out, his jacket soaked and saltwater dripping off his curly wet hair and into his face.

After getting the boat tied up, he yelled at us with a sense of urgency, as the wind blew in gusts around us, "Dese boxes are vet and coming apart! Stand dere and I'll try to hand dem to you."

But as he lifted the sodden cardboard from the water-filled bottom of the dory and tried to hand us the first box, the contents spilled partly in the wet dory and partly on the sandy beach that was rapidly disappearing under mounting breakers. Charlie waded in the shallow water to the skiff and helped Hans get out all the rest of the water- soaked boxes, holding them together with only partial success, while the children and I gathered what we could that bobbed around us in the water, before floating further and further away.

As I gathered the water damaged school supplies together on our home-made table I felt frustrated with our situation.

"Why didn't you stay in town till the weather let up!" It wasn't a question. I was upset.

Hans, not the pacifier Charlie was, replied, "I thought you vanted the kids' books so dey could get started vit der school vork. So I brought dem."

I knew him well enough to know that weather was no deciding factor when he had a job to do. Maybe that was why he was often in demand on fishing boats.

I saw the large assortment of water-logged books, workbooks, and writing paper, and other damaged supplies that the homeschool program had sent, not to mention what might also be floating out in the bay or sinking to the bottom. I know everyone else was upset; I was just the most expressive. "These boxes are ruined. Now what are we going to do. They were late getting here as it is."

Charlie said, "Just relax (he used that word often). I know it will take a long time to get more school supplies from Juneau, so why don't we just let the kids go to the village school? They could walk along the beach on good days and Hans or I can take them on the bad days, then pick them up after school. Maybe when the weather gets real bad we can come up with some money to rent the cabin in town."

He seldom expressed his own frustration. Though he tried to calm me down, what he proposed was somewhat unrealistic, but it was better than no plan. Becky and Malcolm were already a couple of weeks late getting started with their eighth and fifth grade classes.

I agreed that was probably the best solution for the time being. Becky and Malcolm had big smiles in spite of the mess in front of them; they missed their village playmates. Now they would get to see their friends more often.

I boxed what I could of the books and supplies and got them ready to send back to Juneau with a letter of explanation. I presumed all the Juneau office could do was throw everything away, but I felt it was better if they saw the damage, since I didn't think they would be happy about what had happened.

The next day Charlie, Becky, Malcolm, and I took the dory in to town when it was light enough and the waves had settled down a little and for

The winter of '68, during Nov. and Dec., we had lots of snow. The barn is to the right with the remnants of the Whaling Station along the beach in the background.

The winter of '68 was hard on the sheep, too. They no longer needed to be fenced as they stayed close to our cabin. Sugar, always on duty when the sheep were around, kept a watchful eye out for foxes.

the second time enrolled the children in the Akutan Elementary School. Max gave the class something to occupy them then led us to the adjoining apartment and filled the necessary enrollment papers. When he was finished, he took the two children into the classroom and assigned them desks. I heard welcoming voices saying, "Hi, Becky. Hi, Malcolm." They sounded as happy to see my children as mine were to see them. I started to have a good feeling about the decision, though putting it in place and making it work probably wouldn't be easy. In retrospect, of all the schools they had been in before or even since, that year with Max proved to be one of their best, and most productive. Max was a gifted teacher, and with the help of Sue, his wife, provided a great educational experience for them.

We soon discovered, however, that the plan for them to get back and forth to school was going to present a tremendous challenge. Early every morning we would get the kids up to send them on their two mile journey in the semidarkness on the beach walk to school. The weather in the fall was often rainy and sometimes stormy. Many times they would arrive at the school house late and drenched. The beach rocks between the village and the head of the bay were usually covered with green slippery moss so it could be tricky walking on them, trying to keep their footing without falling down. When I use the word 'beach', I'm not referring to a dry wide sandy beach. That beach was narrow and the sand was always wet, as the tide came right up to those moss-covered rocks, never allowing the sand to dry. It wouldn't have mattered; the wind and the rain would have taken care of that. Besides arriving at school with their clothes soaked through, there were days when it was too stormy for Becky and Malcolm to even go by boat. Getting them to and from school had become a major problem. However, we had other more serious problems facing us by now.

Chapter

20

Thanksgiving

$\mathcal{By}\ \mathcal{November}$ of '69 our food box was almost empty, which was no surprise. There wasn't a whole lot in it to begin with as I struggled to put together daily meals for six hungry people. We tried to live off the land as much as possible but there were still gaps in our diet. With no more fuel for the two gas lanterns, they sat in the storage half of the cabin. Though the oil stove was perpetually on, we ran it so low the carburetor kept carboning up. Also it got clogged with the dregs that sat in the bottom of the oil drum since we had to tip it when it got lighter and lighter on the stand. I now could add cleaning carburetors to my resume.' I hoped a fishing boat would show up before we ran completely out and would want to trade a little oil for anything we had left that they might want. We had some white household candles that we used sparingly in the evenings for limited light and blew them out early. I felt sort of like I was hibernating, and maybe I was.

Daylight now came so late the children would have had to make the beach journey in the dark, so Charlie or Hans ran them in, and now that money and boat gas were so limited, whoever took them in just stayed in town visiting while waiting for school to end. Then on a plane day in mid-November, Charlie brought our mail when he came home with the children. There was a welcome surprise.

A friend of mine, Babe Blue, the former hospital administrator at Seward General Hospital when I was Director of Nurses, sent us what used to be referred to as a CARE package, one sent to people in need. The box was filled with an assortment of groceries that included a small can of Vienna sausages. I decided to save them for our Thanksgiving meal as a treat, the only item on our plates that might be a break in our monotonous menu. The other items included such staples as sugar, flour, coffee, tea, and powdered milk (not the lumpy kind). Babe and I had kept in touch occasionally since I'd embarked on my 'great adventure,' though I was too embarrassed to let her know how badly the ranch was failing and how dire our circumstances had become. Somehow, she read between the lines and sent that food-filled package, the only one we received from anyone in all the time we were there. We now had some variety in our diet of mutton, sea lion liver, and dried blueberries.

As the days became colder, the coldest November in our memory, with lots of snow and strong winds, we sold what animals we could to the villagers and fishing boats, mostly 'on the hoof.' Most of the money we received went for heating oil and gas for the dory.

Becky and Malcolm must have been aware of our dire situation, though we tried not to discuss it in front of them, and told them things were going to get better once Charlie and Hans got fishing jobs; we were just having a temporary setback. I was glad they were able to go to school most days and be in a warm classroom, and be fed the nutritious beans, rice, and cheese that the USDA provided. Oh yes, and Stark powdered milk.

When Thanksgiving Day rolled around, it didn't really feel like a holiday as I moved about in the limited light from the small window over the tiny kitchen sink. But I reminded myself that we were all together, unlike several other Thanksgivings. I prepared a small meal with what was still in the CARE box and opened the little can of sausages. When I had the meager fare assembled, we gathered on our narrow beds, which were pushed close to the stove, and in the flickering light of several candles we ate the skimpy holiday meal.

There were seven tiny sausages in the can, and after I handed out one small sausage apiece, I said, "Eric's the youngest so I think he needs more nourishment." No one objected when I gave the extra one to him. We were a quiet group sitting there in the late afternoon gloom, which mirrored our thoughts.

The near silence was interrupted by the sound of an engine. We all jumped up and went to the front window and in the fading light saw a skiff pull up onto our beach. Two figures climbed out and headed for our cabin. As they drew closer we recognized Peter Stepetin and Tommy McGlashan, two of the most helpful people we knew, guys we could always call on if we needed assistance. What could they be doing here late in the day on this special holiday?

When they entered the candle-lit room, Peter, in his usual outspoken way said, "What you doin' sittin' around in the dark for? We came to invite you to a party. There's a fishing boat in town and those guys brought turkeys and lots of food."

Then Tommy spoke up. "The party's at my house. There's all kinds of stuff. We came to get you guys."

"Vell, come on guys, let's go!" Hans shouted with enthusiasm.

It didn't take us long to put on boots and grab our jackets. As we followed Pete and Tommy into town in our dory, I felt grateful that we were being included in their feast.

When we entered Tommy's house, I immediately smelled roast turkey and sage, mixed with other aromas that knotted my hungry stomach even more. Men, women, and children jammed the room, all talking at once, most of them standing and balancing plates of food. As we peeled off our jackets, I heard voices shout, "Hi, Charlie! Hi, guys. Come on in. Grab a plate."

Tommy's cheerful young wife, Irene, smiled as she ushered all of us to a long table covered with plates of sliced turkey, potatoes, corn, and other vegetables, plus several still uncut pumpkin pies—mostly what one would expect at a Thanksgiving feast. Even though we were the last to arrive there was lots of food remaining.

"Help yourselves. We got plenty," Irene said enthusiastically, which made us feel welcome. I was a little ashamed that we three adults had allowed our lives to take such a downward turn. Some tough decisions, though yet unsaid, were practically hanging in the air. The contrast of the two Thanksgiving meals tended to clarify the situation we were in. But this was not the time to dwell on it.

While I stood with a plate of food and visited with my village neighbors, I had flashes of returning to the head of the bay when the party was over—to the cold dark cabin and its dwindling food supply. The isolated life there had provided the comfort that solitude brings as a retreat from the world, an opportunity to learn more about one's self. But I was beginning to accept that I was more of a social being than I had thought. I finally realized how much I had missed my life in the village. I had believed that my love for Akutan was because of our life at the head of the bay, living in a place we had built ourselves, primitive as it was. But isolation can only hold its charm for so long, then I think man's nature starts to yearn for the companionship of others. Maybe that's how villages are formed. It means giving up a bit of one's independent streak, in order to meet one's social needs but it was now clear to me that the village life on that island was the greater source of my happiness. If we'd had the money to restock and if we'd received our 'home site', I can't know if I would have had this epiphany.

When I finished eating, I thanked Irene for her hospitality, and visited with Anesia, soft spoken and serious, somehow exuding a kind and motherly personality. She was well-suited in her role as village medical aide. Agnes McGlashan Feller also stopped in, and I talked with her for a bit. She was Uncle Paul's and Uncle Bill's younger sister, in her early fifties. She lived in the large two story house next to the school, with the marine radio and the post office room. She brought me up to date on the various happenings in the village as I hadn't been able to make it into town much for a while since we limited the use of our boat. As much as I enjoyed the great meal, I realized that it wasn't only the food that I had missed. What was almost the bleakest Thanksgiving in my memory became one of my most unforgettable.

When we were ready to leave and head back up the bay, Charlie went outside to check the weather, as we knew the wind had started to pick up a little when we came to town. When he came back in he told me the waves were a lot bigger and it would be a pretty rough trip home in the dark. He and Hans had made those trips many times over the years, but he didn't really like taking the children and me out in it. I was in complete agreement. Agnes Feller heard our predicament and came up to me.

"Joan, why don't all of you spend the night at my place? I have extra bedrooms."

We accepted her hospitality without hesitation. During the night the weather worsened and by morning there were gale-force winds churning the waters, which made the bay too hazardous for travel. Aggie generously told us we could stay as long as we needed.

She also provided meals for us, which we appreciated more than she realized. She had no way of knowing the survival diet we had been on. The abundance of food available to us now reinforced my feelings of how bad our situation had become. Every morning for breakfast, there was warm homemade bread that we covered with real butter from a round yellow tin plus homemade blueberry jam, which was a treat. Somehow, when I saw that jam it stirred up some smoldering emotions—anger and resentment, to name a few. We had blueberry bushes near our cabin but no money to buy sugar to make jam. Why did three people with marketable job skills let their situation deteriorate from ownership of five hundred animals to an inability to buy a sack of sugar? Enough was enough. I had already begun to think of the ranch in the past tense. Charlie's earlier depression was now more understandable.

As the November storm continued, Becky and Malcolm enjoyed playing with their friends and all of us enjoyed sleeping in real beds in warm rooms. During this time I got to know Aggie on a more personal level, though she had always been friendly to my family and me. As the storm began to dissipate I made preparations to return to the cabin, though without much enthusiasm knowing what awaited us—not much. Then, without being aware of our devastating circumstances, Aggie surprised me. She entered the bedroom we'd been staying in as I was changing the linens.

"Joan, my family and I would like to spend a few months in Anchorage this winter but I need someone to take over the post office and the weather report for Reeve Aleutian Airways. I know you have your place at the head of the bay, but it'll be a lot easier for your kids to get to school if you stay in town. You could all stay here and house sit. Charlie and Hans could go up to the cabin and take care of things if they need to and Charlie could look after the AC generator here. It has to be kept running all the time because of the radio."

She had worked this all out in her mind before approaching me with her offer. While many of the local people were aware of how badly the ranch had deteriorated, its status actually having bypassed 'farm' and gone straight to subsistence living, I could tell she was unaware of how extreme our needs had become. In all the years we had lived at Akutan, Aggie had never been to our cabin. If she had she would know she didn't have to convince me to accept her offer. I was almost speechless with amazement at the turn of events, but I managed to get a few words out. "Of course, I'll do it. I'd be happy to."

The marine radio, the only emergency link to the outside world, half the size of a refrigerator, was located in a small room and available to the local people to send messages. Aggie also used it when she gave the weather report to Reeve Aleutian Air when they notified her they planned to bring in mail and sometimes passengers, if the Goose could get in. That was usually every two or three weeks. Though giving the weather report was a nonpaying job, getting to house sit was more than sufficient compensation.

Then she told me about her other job, the paying one. "Since I'm the postmistress, I can't just leave the post office duties without someone to look after things. If you agree to house sit and take care of the weather report, could I submit an application for you to take over the temporary postmistress position? It shouldn't take long to hear from them. Then your family could move in and my family could leave. So what do you think?"

I couldn't wait for my brain to finish processing my good fortune. I quickly replied, "I'll be glad to help out, Aggie. The children will love being in town with their friends, plus being able to walk to school in just a few minutes and arrive with dry clothes."

She laughed at that, but I'm not sure she realized I wasn't exaggerating, that it was the second worst problem that had faced us. Hunger was the first.

"What about Charlie and Hans? Do you have to check with them first?"

Hell, no, I thought. I don't have to check with them about anything.

They wanted the ranch; we lost it—and over fifty thousand dollars in the process. Now it's my turn to have what I want, to live in this village. I always loved it here, and so did Becky and Malcolm.

"No, Aggie, they'll be happy to have us stay in town. To be honest, things are a bit rough out there this time of year. And you must know the ranch has not turned out the way we'd expected. Hans and Charlie make much better fishermen." That was only half true.

She said she would submit my application right away as they hoped to spend Christmas in Anchorage. I hoped to spend mine in a warm, well-lighted house.

I thanked Aggie for the welcome offer. I had lived through some dark hours of almost no food or money while struggling to care for three young children, but like so many crazy things that had happened to me on that island, everything continued to work out for the best.

Aggie and her family left as soon as I got my postal approval and we moved into her house shortly before Christmas. Becky and Malcolm were as excited as I was as they gathered their things from the dark cold cabin and moved into the spacious well-lighted house with their own bedrooms. My own favorite features were the indoor toilet (especially now that there was snow on the ground) and a bathtub that wasn't round and silver. I could even use my long buried waffle iron after all, along with the other almost forgotten appliances. Compared to our cabin, Aggie's house was like a five star hotel.

They must have known there was no turning back but Charlie and Hans accepted her offer as willingly as I did, though I felt a bit sorry for them. Their only job was to look after the big AC generator. I made waffles our first day after Aggie's family left.

21

Back in the Village

After I helped with the move into Aggie's house and took a short time to look over my new jobs, I went next door to the school-house with Becky and Malcolm. From now on, I assured the Meekers, the children should have regular attendance. Since Becky was in the eighth grade, I was glad she had such a dedicated teacher as Max to prepare her for the transition to high school. Malcolm was in fifth by then, and was doing well. By the time Aggie came back I hoped to have enough saved from my post office pay check to rent Uncle Paul's cabin again so the children could remain in town for the remainder of the school year.

My postal duties involved sorting the mail and putting it in a few slots every two or three weeks when the plane showed up. Also, I opened the outside door for short scheduled periods so the residents could mail packages, buy stamps, and take care of other postal needs. And, of course, there were always government forms to fill out. None of my duties took very long though, and happily I found myself yet again in charge of myself, at least locally. That is, no one was standing over me telling me what to do. I'm a bit independent that way.

My other job was monitoring the big marine radio—which was NOT in a closed up room. It squawked all the time. My main duty was the weather report which I gave on the days the Goose wanted to try to get in since it had to deal with various weather elements, such as fog, waves, and wind. The pilot needed to know how high the ceiling was; that is, if the usual fog had lifted sufficiently for the plane to get under it, and how big the waves were, because if the bay was too choppy the plane couldn't land. When I took over that job, I was told the visual guidelines to use in order to determine the weather conditions. There were particular locations on the high hill across the bay where the number of feet could be determined as to how low the cloud cover was, for example. My unscientific report was actually pretty easy. There were marginal days when I hated to be the bad guy and give an unfavorable report based on what was going on at the time, only to have the fog lift a few hours later with the winter sun peeking through. But both the pilot and I took the weather seriously, so we missed an occasional plane day.

With the school situation taken care of, I began to enjoy village life again after so much isolation at the head of the bay. I was reminded of my first year in Akutan, with lots of visiting back and forth, plus many birthday parties to attend. The population still ranged around ninety, and since everyone was invited to the birthdays, there was lots of socializing, feasting on various desserts. It was so different from the way I had lived for quite a while. Sometimes I would go as long as a month at the head of the bay without seeing anyone but my immediate family, especially when we had some rather lengthy storms.

Now as we sat in the comfort of a real house, warm and well lighted that December of '69, Charlie, Hans and I had a long overdue family conference. There had been too many setbacks, with the stock disasters and limited income from our investment, besides bad fishing seasons. All that remained were a small herd of cows over in Hot Springs Bay that had proved self-sufficient and a few sheep at the head of the bay that stayed near the cabin. All the pigs and chickens had been sold or eaten.

We agreed to notify BLM right after Christmas that we could no longer keep the grazing lease, partly due to animal losses and lack of funds, and partly due to the Land Claims, which was looking more and more like a done deal. We also couldn't afford to live at Uncle Paul's with no guaranteed income, so Charlie decided to check with Standard Oil and see about working at Dutch Harbor again. If not, he thought of exploring the Anchorage market. He hadn't had much success with fishing, so he no longer even considered that.

The three of us felt a sense of relief once we made that final decision. The ranch hadn't turned out as planned but we had no regrets about that decision. We'd had lots of time to adjust to our circumstances. We would never have found that special island that brought all of us so much happiness had it not been for our desire to start a ranch. But our unpreparedness was almost laughable. Most outsiders looking in could have easily seen that our venture was doomed no matter what. I'm thankful that we were too naïve to see it.

Charlie and Hans took the dory up to the head of the bay on most days and did what work they could. Winter had set in with snow on the ground, but there were still some sheep left that they planned to butcher eventually, so they wanted to keep checking on them. Also, there was still a certain amount of wrapping up to do with our things in the cabin. They put what they could in boxes and brought them to town, where I kept them at Aggie's till we moved into Uncle Paul's. We also began selling some of our things to the villagers.

We spent that last Christmas in the village, which we looked forward to, remembering our wonderful experiences that first year at the schoolhouse. The processor Deep Sea from Wakefield Fisheries at Kodiak Island was tied up at the other end of the village, but as Christmas approached it shut down and left a small maintenance crew on board over the holidays. The cook also wanted to leave for a short time, just between planes, so the skipper asked if I would cook a few of the evening meals, including fixing the crew a turkey for Christmas. He said there were just six men and they could get their own breakfast and lunch in an informal way. Since my postal and weather report duties revolved around a plane planning to try and make it in, I had lots of free days. One of the perks of the Deep Sea cooking job was a free turkey that the skipper told me I could have for our own dinner, a nice change from mutton. Again I actually enjoyed my cooking duties, even though it was just a small group of men. They had a large amount of food supplies in their pantry and freezer, so I wouldn't have to be as creative as I'd had to be back in our cabin.

With the winter snows, sledding was a fun activity that village life provided. A long steep hill was behind the school, and once the snow stuck it was a favorite location for the kids. Like many of the others, Becky and Malcolm used large flattened pasteboard boxes for sleds and enjoyed incredible sledding that winter. As soon as school was out, even with little daylight, the children grabbed their pasteboard sleds and slowly trudged up that imposing hill. They dug their boots into the snow till they were tired of climbing, then placed their homemade sleds down on the packed snow, laid face down on them and clung to the sides as they swiftly flew down the hillside, only to repeat the long climb up.

In late winter Agnes and her family returned and she reclaimed that comfortable house and her old jobs. So it was back to DC current and the limited space in Uncle Paul's. But I was happy we were able to afford to remain in the village. Becky and Malcolm liked having playmates, though they had clearly enjoyed the carefree life at the head of the bay. There were advantages to both lifestyles. I'm glad they were able to experience both.

Though they weren't sold in Akutan, comic books were another favorite among the children. Sergie, the older bachelor who took Opal up to our cabin on her arrival, kept a box of comics inside his door, alongside a chair. When he made the forty mile trip by skiff to Unalaska to get various supplies from Carl's Commercial, the big general store, Sergie always brought back more comics. He generously shared them with his visitors, so I could usually find Malcolm sitting in Sergie's cabin with a group of boys, all engrossed in the latest reading material.

One day a baby sea lion showed up on the town beach. Some local dogs were barking at it and it tried to bite at them to keep them at bay. Peter Stepetin rescued it from the dogs and got it into his house nearby. He kept it as a pet for a short time and Becky and Malcolm enjoyed seeing the little sea lion close up, not a common sight outside of a zoo. Eventually, he returned the little sea mammal to its natural habitat, the icy waters in the bay, before it became a meal for someone.

We had our own pet, Sugar. After we moved to Uncle Paul's she was given a designated spot by the kitchen door—the only door- and I made her a little bed with an old blanket. Since she was an outside dog, I brought her in late in the day and she curled up on her blanket, as the kitchen was small. However, it wasn't her spot of choice. In the evening while I cooked dinner and the guys sat and talked, I watched her out of the corner of my eye as she frequently slid out of her own space by the door, then crawled on her belly at the rate of no more than three inches a minute. She headed for the space behind the oil cook stove, a place she knew she was not supposed to be. If I said her name sharply, she scampered back to her place by the door. But sometimes I pretended not to notice as she moved slowly, occasionally stealing a glance my way without turning her head. It was good for her morale that she thought she won once in a while.

But there was a time when I didn't find her behavior quite so amusing. I had cut up a chicken and baked it in the oven, then set the pan on the open oven door till we were ready to eat. Sugar quietly made it to the oven, and then quickly grabbed a drumstick out of the pan. I hollered "Sugar!" but she didn't drop her prize, just made for the outside door, which I opened for her while shouting, "Bad dog!" She knew she was in trouble, though usually she was quite obedient. I guess the smell of baked chicken lowered her defenses. I'm glad she didn't know how tasty those chickens were all those years she protected them from foxes. Actually, a baked drumstick beats a raw one covered with feathers any day. However, she didn't try that little trick again, maybe because I didn't tempt her with food on the oven door anymore.

After I resettled in Uncle Paul's cabin I let the local people know I was available to give them any help they needed with income taxes, which soon would be due. I had previously taken courses in tax preparation so I had a fairly good background. They knew there was no charge for any assistance I might give; they had been generous to me in so many ways. I've already mentioned how they gave me fish, baked goods and casseroles. Some took me up on my tax help offer, as the forms were not always easy to interpret. Also, I knew a few of the older villagers could not read, having lived through the internment days with very limited educational facilities.

About that time, a boy about four years old came to stay with us for a short time as he and his three young siblings had lost both their parents in separate incidents. His mother was Pete Stepetin's sister and his father had been a friend of ours. The four children were now orphans so the villagers had to make arrangements for them to be taken in by families. His name was Mike, though he went by Mikey, and he was a very cheerful little preschooler. Eric liked having a playmate closer to his age than his brother and sister, so he enjoyed having a live-in companion. Though we were in the tiny village cabin, he didn't take up much space, and it seemed there was always room for one more. One time when I made a pumpkin pie Mikey liked it so much he wanted seconds, so I let him have two pieces, young as he was. Hans asked me, "Do you tink he'll get sick?" But Mikey didn't. Later on, when he went to live at Anesia's, we missed his lively presence.

The approach of spring heralded the Easter season, which was observed with the villagers' own traditions. The men gave the small white Russian Orthodox Church a thorough cleaning in preparation for the coming event. That included the beautiful red carpeting, for which they borrowed my vacuum cleaner that year, one of our various useless items that we brought on the *Robert Eugene.* Someone had a portable generator so they could operate the vacuum. Fuma, another older bachelor, took care of the little church on a regular basis. His appearance was unique in that he wore a black eye patch, but having only one eye did not hinder him from keeping the solid red plush carpet in great condition. He was known to clean spots and pick up lint on his hands and knees, so I was happy to be in the village that Easter with the vacuum cleaner. Finally, it had a purpose for being there. Fuma was a gentle soft-spoken man who loved cats and kept a houseful of them. I was told they were all as well taken care of as the village church.

The women had their own traditional duties. They had been saving empty coffee cans for a while, one pound sizes and larger, in preparation for Easter baking. Other types of cans were also saved since there weren't a large amount of coffee cans available. Tea was more commonly drunk in the village. A few days before Easter Sunday they made large batches of bread dough, often with nuts and/or citrus pieces added, and then placed balls of the dough in the greased cans to rise. Once the dough reached the top of the cans they were placed in the stoves to bake. As the dough continued to rise when exposed to the oven heat, it formed a dome above the can, not unlike the onion domes Russian churches are noted for. That type of coffee cake was called kulich. When removed from the cans, they were iced and set aside.

On Easter Sunday they exchanged many of them with their neighbors, and since we were again villagers, we received a bountiful supply of kulich, which was especially delicious when toasted and buttered, though not in an AC toaster, but in a skillet on the stove. Because each household had made so many kuliches and because they were beginning to harden, for the next few days afterward we observed children having 'kulich wars', throwing the hardened coffee cakes at each other. Remnants lined the grass on both sides of the boardwalk during Easter Week. The seagulls were happy.

The sound of the melodious church bell ringing on Easter Sunday added to the holiday atmosphere. The large bell was off limits to the children except on that special day when they were allowed to ring it at will. So for a large part of the day a loud ringing sound could be heard in the background of all the socializing, and small groups of children hung out at the church waiting their turn. The children wore their best clothes that day, the girls in dresses instead of the pants that were usually worn, the boys in long sleeve shirts and suit jackets, all dressed up running up and down the boardwalk, so happy in their new clothes. Becky and Malcolm wore theirs, though they'd almost outgrown them.

For our family this was to be our last Easter celebration in Akutan, so we visited as many families as we could. We were able to put aside thoughts of the unwanted changes that would be happening to us very soon, as we enjoyed that holiday with all our friends. It was also to be our last happy time together as a family before leaving Akutan.

Chapter

22

An Ending
and a Beginning

That spring we scraped together the money to make the final payment on our five year agricultural loan. Was there something significant in them setting it at five years? Had they made this loan before to would-be ranchers? Did they have some prior knowledge about such undertakings? We were broke but thankfully we wouldn't be in debt. We hoped to start over in a different direction—definitely not ranching—with a clean slate.

I boxed things that we wouldn't need before we left in the late spring. There was no feeling of excitement, no anticipation that we were returning to some of the comforts we had left behind. The five of us (Eric was too young to have such thoughts) had come to enjoy a simpler, slower-paced life. We felt we would never choose city life again unless there was a very necessary reason, but we didn't expect to find another Akutan. This special life would be what we had salvaged from our aborted ranching attempt.

We put some things aside for sale and notified the villagers to stop by Uncle Paul's and check out the items. It helped to thin out our belongings and gave us a little cash, which we greatly needed. As friends stopped by we shared a cup of tea and I told them I would be back, that we just had to get back on our feet financially. We also had to get Becky into high school, and eventually Malcolm, so I was being a bit unrealistic. I just couldn't handle the reality that I was leaving.

Hans began his own preparations to leave Akutan for the last time as he got ready to head for Bristol Bay for the salmon season as a deckhand for his previous year's employer. Now that his ranching days had come to an end, he decided to stay with fishing. Having done it for a few years now, he realized that he preferred it to ranching or painting. He had the right qualifications: good with boats and little fear of rough water. Though our ranch partnership ended, he remained part of our family, making his home with us for many years. Hans would always be Charlie's and my best friend, and a loving, caring second father to Becky, Malcolm, Eric and our two later additions.

In early May Charlie and I hauled some of our boxes to the head of the bay and stored them in the barn, then padlocked it. Then we put our furniture and some boxes in the front part of our cabin. I held plywood in place as Charlie nailed it over the two cabin windows, then closed the padlock on our homemade door. As I stood there and watched him snap that lock on that gloomy May afternoon I felt the finality and knew it was over but I couldn't accept it. It would be months before I would be able to convince myself that we weren't coming back. Sometimes there're things we know but we aren't ready to face. At least I wasn't. Charlie was always a reserved person when it came to his feelings so he seldom let on how he felt, whether good or bad. He kept it all inside, but I was sure he shared my feelings of sadness as we walked back to the dory for the last time, leaving behind the home where we had naively thought we would be spending the rest of our lives.

Back in the village, Charlie radioed Standard Oil at Dutch Harbor to see if they had any work for him that summer, since that had always been their busiest time. They not only wanted him to start immediately, that early May of '70, but told him his old position as petroleum operator had come up and they had not picked a replacement yet. They offered the job to him since he was already familiar with it, though he'd been gone five and a half years 'checking out the grass on the other side', which certainly wasn't greener. Family housing, however, would not be available till July, though there was a room available for him to rent. After telling the kids and me good-by he left on a fishing boat for Dutch Harbor, taking Sugar, with him, plus some of our things, which was a big help. He or Hans hoped to come back over and get the rest of our stored things once we had a place to live there.

With their departure, I felt as if my life on Akutan was ending too abruptly, like the cord was finally cut and I'd soon enter another world, another life. I still had lots to do with Becky's graduation fast approaching and getting money together so we could leave. I continued to sell what I could and finally decided to contact my dad for help. I had not seen him since Eric was four days old, so I put in a marine radio call, the kind parents frequently get. If he would help with the very expensive air fares, I wanted to visit him.

My father, a retired widower, who lived alone, agreed to help me. I made reservations for June 1, the day the scheduled plane was due, a month short of five years to the day that we arrived at Akutan with such great expectations of a new life. While it was not the life we had looked forward to, we were happier there than any place we lived before or since, and I know I speak for all of us.

Leaving Akutan was difficult, but giving up the ranch turned out to be one of our wiser decisions. Later, we learned of the outcome of the Native Claims. The government underestimated the dogged persistence and intellectual capabilities of the Native lawyers. On December 23, 1971, President Richard M. Nixon signed into law The Alaska Native Claims Settlement Act. If we had found a way to increase our stock, it still would have been futile. There was now no possibility of receiving a home site with BLM, and the lease program would be changing.

As we climbed aboard the Goose that June for the last time, I knew we had all experienced a unique place at a unique time in the island's history. There would be no Brown dynasty remaining, but a small herd of inbred Hereford cattle would continue to do their part to keep the memories of Hans Radtke, Charlie and Joan Brown, and their children, Becky, Malcolm and Eric, alive as long as there would be those who would be curious enough to inquire how those wild cows came to be on Akutan Island.

Epilogue

$\mathcal{B}ecky\ completed$ high school in three years and after her graduation at Unalaska High School in May, 1973, at age sixteen, the children and I moved to the small town of Homer on the mainland. Charlie stayed on at Dutch Harbor till '75 when he received a transfer to Kenai, less than one hundred miles from us.

We picked Homer as I wanted easier access to medical facilities for our growing family, now four children and another on the way. Homer's other attractions included dirt roads, no traffic lights, no house numbers, no street signs—my kind of place—a **really** small town. However, like Akutan it was not spared and over the years the old Homer ceased to exist.

Becky received a scholarship to the University of Alaska, and earned a degree in Business Administration. That knowledge helped her develop a successful career as the owner of a unique and popular toy store in Homer, which she's operated for many years. She holds fond memories of her caring Uncle Hansie and her happy childhood growing up in the Aleutians. During my moments of nostalgia, I see her running up and down that narrow village boardwalk, flaming red hair streaming in the wind, accompanied by laughing playmates with which she has remained lifelong friends.

Malcolm, having developed an early interest in the Aleut heritage, received a BA in Anthropology from the University of Alaska. Later he completed his Master's in Public Administration with a 4.0 average, as he became interested in governments and how they can improve their communities, especially the small ones. He's held various positions from planning director to city manager in towns and native villages in Alaska as he never lost his love of remote places, a carry-over from his childhood spent in the storm-ridden Aleutians. Like Becky, he retains friendships that were formed in those too brief years in the Chain. He also joined the Army National Guard and after twenty -seven years of service my little 'David' of the pig farm of long ago retired as Major Malcolm Brown, having received that promotion while stationed in the mid-east. The then governor of Alaska, Sarah Palin, made her first overseas journey when she flew to Kuwait to make that presentation to him.

Eric's proclivity for drawing pictures on our cabin's cardboard walls was a forerunner of his emerging talent as a theater set designer. Predictably, he received his Bachelor's Degree in Theater from the University of Alaska. His designs were so realistic that when he offered to build me a house I knew he meant two dimensional. I'd seen his stage 'couches' that looked so real that if one attempted to sit that person would slide to the floor. Now Eric is a theater tech for all the schools in the Anchorage School District. As mentioned earlier, he still retains his barn door scar, from that inquisitive incident.

Like towns, over time my family increased in size to include Ben in '71 and Sam in '74. Unlike with towns, I welcomed that expansion.

Ben followed in his father's footsteps—no, not as a rancher! He became a petroleum operator, Charlie's more successful occupation. He also inherited Charlie's ability to make friends with everyone he met. When I would meet new people I frequently found myself saying, "I'm Ben Brown's mother," and the usual response was, "I know Ben." I used to say, "I'm Charlie Brown's wife," and got the same response. I doubt either ever said, "I'm Joan Brown's husband/ son." But maybe I'm selling myself short because someone on Akutan and in the Homer Post Office remembered Joan Brown and now I've entered a new period in my life.

Sam, our youngest, has no memory of the Aleutians as he was only six days old when I took him from Homer to Dutch Harbor on a snowy day in January, 1974, to spend time with Charlie. My attitude about taking newborns to a remote area about eight hundred miles from doctors and hospitals had changed somewhat from my earlier feelings about returning to the Aleutians when Eric was less than a year old. I returned to Dutch Harbor so soon after Sam's birth as I hoped to strengthen our sometimes fragile family ties, and felt separations were not helpful.

Unlike my other four who call Alaska home, Sam preferred to wander, and equipped with an uncanny ability to learn languages numbering into the teens, he received his degree in linguistics and settled in South Korea to teach.

Hans, having satisfied his ranch yearnings such as they were, also gave up house painting and spent the rest of his summers fishing Bristol Bay for salmon. He remained a part of our family, Charlie's and my best friend, and continued to help raise our five children in his role as third parent.

Plagued by hypertension and diabetes, complicated by liver problems, Hans died in 1996 in an Anchorage hospital. When I notified the children that his condition had worsened and death was imminent, all five dropped what they were doing and left for Anchorage within hours of my call.

Becky and Ben came from Homer, over two hundred miles away, Eric drove three hundred sixty miles from Fairbanks, and Malcolm and Sam flew in from Albuquerque, New Mexico. We had shared a lot as a family and it was hard for all of us to accept that after thirty-three years he would no longer be a part of it. When Hans died, Charlie's emotional barrier cracked and he broke into uncontrolled sobbing, which I had only witnessed once before in the forty-one years we'd been together, when his mother died. Hans was only sixty-one years old, but had lived his dreams, accomplished much and had been greatly loved by his adopted family.

One and a half years later, Charlie was diagnosed with pancreatic cancer. When told he was terminal he took it in stride, maybe hardened by all the other setbacks he had encountered in his life. He remained a calm, cheerful person. As his disease spread, a Seattle cancer specialist told him he had about two weeks remaining. True to his calm and outwardly cheerful nature,

Charlie smiled at me and said, "Let's go to Homecoming!" which was at Silver City, New Mexico the next week. The following morning we were on a plane to Western New Mexico University, where we had met forty-four years before. After homecoming, we headed for Arizona and a new oncologist who helped him survive three more months to enjoy his favorite activity, visiting with people.

As his condition worsened, he grew weaker, but when asked said he had little pain, just discomfort. However, he had seldom been a complainer, so I could only know what he told me. Though he had suffered through a damaging depression during the early ranch period, he never showed that side again. But he still preferred to keep his inner feelings to himself, often maintaining an easy-going demeanor, reverting to his old 'what, me worry' image.

Charlie loved telling funny stories to anyone who would listen, which included the ambulance attendant while he was being driven through Tucson streets with lights flashing, after his heart had stopped briefly in the doctor's office. When I pulled up behind the ambulance at the emergency entrance, the rear doors opened and I was surprised to see a smiling patient who'd just had a near death experience, being wheeled out by a laughing attendant. That was the Charlie I knew. He had been a good balance for Hans' more serious nature and my more emotional one. He died December 6, 1999, on an oncology ward in Tucson, Arizona, a faint smile even in that last hour. He was buried in Homer, Alaska, one lot removed from his best friend Hans, now his partner forever. The lot in between has been reserved for me.

I've had an assortment of short term occupations such as a substitute teacher, art editor for a local paper, bookkeeper, tax preparer, medical examiner for insurance companies, and artist. I also worked as a real estate broker for many years, which played a part in Doug finding me. That occupation, his curiosity and the remarkable endurance of some cows resulted in this book.